FINDING
Happiness
Within

7 Lessons
on Life,
Love,
Hope, and
Transcendental
Meditation

OLIVIA LOPEZ

BALBOA.PRESS
A DIVISION OF HAY HOUSE

Balboa Press books may be ordered through booksellers or by contacting:

Balboa Press
A Division of Hay House
1663 Liberty Drive
Bloomington, IN 47403
www.balboapress.com
844-682-1282

Print information available on the last page.

ISBN: 979-8-7652-3877-6 (sc)
ISBN: 979-8-7652-3876-9 (e)

Balboa Press rev. date: 02/21/2023

I dedicate this book to Maharishi Mahesh Yogi who brought to the world the knowledge of transcending and the experience of profound happiness.

Contents

Acknowledgments

I am grateful to Laurina and Bolton Carroll, my mom and stepdad, and to Dr. Alfred and Dianne Lopez, my dad and stepmom, for their unconditional love and support.

Thank you to all my half siblings for their love and support: Alfred, Stacy, Sarah and Chris.

In loving memory of Stacy Lopez, who passed away. She was always such a loving big sister to me.

Thank you to my amazing boyfriend, Tommy Stirling, who brings me so much happiness and joy. Your love and support mean the world to me.

Thank you to my developmental editor Lisa Thaler for believing in me, helping me write my first book, and for your continued patience.

Thank you to Laurina Carroll for your assistance with research and fact-checking.

Thank you to Victoria Williams for the final edits.

Thank you to my photographer, Kristie Schram for the amazing Photos and Book Design.

Thank you to all my TM students and Friends for believing in me.

Thank you, David Lynch Foundation, for making this technique accessible to those who need it the most through your programs.

Thank you Maharishi Foundation International and TM for Women for giving me the opportunity to teach Transcendental Meditation.

Thank you Maharishi School and Maharishi International University for giving me an invaluable consciousness based education and helping me become the person I am today.

Thank you, Maharishi Mahesh Yogi, for bringing Transcendental Meditation to the world.

Introduction

Nature does not hurry, yet everything is accomplished.

Lao Tzu

I was introduced to TM in utero. I knew Diversity before Diversity was cool.

My name is Olivia Lopez, and a huge part of my life is Transcendental Meditation (TM). I was born in Albuquerque, New Mexico, October 28, 1987, to an Italian Irish Catholic New York mother, Laurina Buro, and a Native American and New Mexican father, Al Lopez. Al taught Laurina TM on July 21, 1986, in La Jolla, California, where he was living at the time. Technically, I was introduced to TM in utero. Meditating moms have an advantage. Laurina said that as a newborn, I slept through most nights and she was less fatigued than she had expected.

At age four, I learned the TM technique for children called

the "word of wisdom" from Al, and have been practicing ever since. (Most children start no younger than five.) Children under ten practice five minutes, twice a day. Adults practice twenty minutes, twice a day.

When I was five, in September 1993, my parents had an amicable separation. Laurina and I left New Mexico for Germany. Laurina chose to live abroad to pursue her professional interests and be among like-minded meditators.

At age ten, all children who are interested can learn the adult TM technique. I couldn't wait to learn, and from my mother, who completed her TM Teacher Training Course (TTC) a few months after my tenth birthday.

Living in Germany was a valuable experience, although, as an immigrant, at times I felt alienated. I did not look like other Germans. Based on my Spanish features, most thought I was of Turkish or Russian descent. I would explain, "I'm an American who has Spanish heritage, but speaks fluent German." Starting in first grade, I was bullied by some classmates. Later, I struggled academically and was too shy to ask for help. Even though I made it through the highest level of the German education system (gymnasium), I still didn't feel smart enough. Looking back now, I shouldn't have been so hard on myself. Nevertheless, at that time it took a toll on my self-esteem.

When I was fifteen, in 2003, Laurina and I left Germany and moved to Fairfield, Iowa, which had and still has the largest TM community in the United States. There are approximately 10,000 residents and around 3,000 of those practice Transcendental Meditation. I felt so at home. I attended the Maharishi School, a private K–12 school where TM is integrated into the curriculum and every subject addresses consciousness and the unified field of quantum physics.

Although our class had its group of girls who had grown up together, they welcomed me. I was never bullied in school again. My experience of social adversity made me want to always be inclusive in any situation and treat everyone with the utmost kindness.

I always dreamed of becoming a fashion designer. In my senior year of high school, I applied to Columbia College in Chicago and the Art Institute of Chicago for fashion design. (Chicago is about 275 miles east of Fairfield.) Both schools accepted me, but I decided to stay in Fairfield. I don't know why exactly; I just had a gut feeling that I needed to stay there. I no longer felt the pull to be in a larger city. Fairfield's nourishing atmosphere was so charming, I didn't want to leave.

I became a TM teacher in 2010 and earned a Master of Business Administration at the Maharishi International

University in 2011. I taught TM coast-to-coast for ten years, and then paused to reassess my life goals.

My pause to reflect coincided with some health challenges and the COVID-19 pandemic that started in March 2020. It proved that our health and well-being are key, and that I wanted to help others more. I became certified as a Life Coach in 2021. I also wrote this book to share my personal story, including how TM is the foundation of my life, and to offer readers seven universal lessons—and forty self-care tips—from my experience and training.

#

In Lesson 1, Growing Up with Transcendental Meditation, I learned that discipline is a practice. TM is built upon the routine of regular, twice-a-day meditation. In Germany and then in Fairfield and later as a TM teacher in schools and with individuals, I thrived on and supported others in this calm and relaxing practice.

In Lesson 2, Moving to Fairfield, Iowa, I found my community. Raised as an only child by a single mother and away from other family, I didn't realize how much I was missing out on until I moved to Fairfield at the age of fifteen. I felt supported and nourished in Iowa. Everywhere I went, there was a friendly, smiling face. I felt welcomed and that I finally belonged.

In Lesson 3, Becoming a TM Teacher, I learned that with focus, anything is possible. Because I never felt smart enough, for a long time, I was insecure about my intellect and my ability to learn. This changed when I was on my TM Teacher Training Course. For five months, I was able to focus on my studies without distraction, and I learned much more easily than I had ever done before. I finally gained more confidence.

In Lesson 4, Teaching TM Coast-to-Coast, I had to be flexible and adaptable. I have taught TM in urban settings throughout California, Florida, Illinois, and Iowa. I learned to be strong and resilient yet flexible and adaptable, in changing climates and across cultures and lifestyles. It was fun yet challenging. Once I settle in, regardless of where I am, I can feel at home.

In Lesson 5, Coming Home, during the pandemic, I learned to understand my needs and ask for support and guidance. I took a huge step back. "Do less, accomplish more" is a basic principle of Maharishi Mahesh Yogi, founder of the TM program in the mid-1950s. Stress and busyness usually don't help us reach our goals any more easily. American culture encourages us to study hard and work hard—even if we lose sleep and sacrifice our well-being. In the long run, this lifestyle can make us sick. From my personal experience, and those I teach and counsel, everyone needs and deserves time for themselves and to access helpful tools to live a less stressful and more balanced life.

In Lesson 6, Let It Be, I learned my greatest, ongoing lesson: let the universe provide the answer. Have you ever wondered why certain things work out and others don't—regardless how much you may pray and focus on something? Well, in my life, I have accomplished a lot so far and had many desires fulfilled effortlessly. Other times, things haven't gone my way or as I had planned. I needed to let God, the universe, or whatever you wish to call one's higher power, help me out of a stressful situation and even at times move me across the country to protect me. Surrender and trust can help us reach our deepest desires and find fulfillment.

In Lesson 7, the Next Chapter is about moving forward in your life, even with uncertainty. I discuss what life coaching is and my journey of becoming a life coach. I summarize the tools I have used to help me in my life.

Finding Happiness Within is my story about connecting with my purpose and the seven lessons on life, love, hope, and Transcendental Meditation that I learned along the way.

I offer forty self-care tips to help you put those lessons into practice in your own life. We will explore TM, Ayurveda, and other powerful tools to understand where you are in your life, what you want to achieve, and how to feel your best.

LESSON 1
Discipline Is a Practice

Growing Up with Transcendental Meditation

> *I believe that the greatest gift you can give your family and the world is a healthy you.*
>
> Joyce Meyer

Take stock of where you are and prioritize the things that are important.

My Italian Catholic mother from Long Island, New York, Laurina Buro, met my Native American Basque Spanish father, Al Lopez, in a Japanese piano bar in Midtown Manhattan in 1986. Both in the US and Japan, it is customary for a business host to bring visitors to a piano bar so they will feel less homesick. Actresses and singers entertain and talk to the patrons by singing and serving them drinks and dinner. Laurina sang in

English and in Japanese, which she learned in order to get the job. Al, living in La Jolla, California at the time, had brought his out-of-town Japanese business associates. Being in business was a far cry from the early Al.

Born in Kansas City, Kansas, and raised in Albuquerque, New Mexico, Al was a rulebreaker in boarding school and later went through a drugs and rock and roll phase like many young people in America in the '60s and '70s. Then, in 1972, while in dental school in Kansas City, he learned Transcendental Meditation at the local TM center.

TM is a simple, mental technique that allows us to experience a very deep state of relaxation, and this experience of relaxation leads to great benefits in daily life, including a reduction in anxiety, an increase in energy, and an improvement in both mental and physical health. Here is how it's described on the TM website, tm.org:

"It's a simple, natural, effortless technique practiced 20 minutes twice each day while sitting comfortably with the eyes closed.

The TM technique allows your active mind to easily settle inward, through quieter levels of thought, until you experience the most silent and peaceful level of your own awareness — pure consciousness."

The TM technique's benefits start right away and keep growing. Hundreds of independent research studies have found major increases in calmness, creativity, energy, clarity of mind, and happiness" (from tm.org).

For over fifty years, Al's been meditating regularly, twice a day for almost two hours practicing TM and its Advanced Techniques. TM changed his life. In 1974, Al became a TM teacher with Maharishi Mahesh Yogi (1918–2008), founder of the TM program in the mid-1950s, most famous in pop culture for his influence on the Beatles and their music in the late '60s.

My parents' worlds and personalities were vastly different. Al was 22 years her senior and already established in his career. He was also married, but in the process of separating from his wife, with whom he had four children.

Laurina was single, living alone, and an aspiring actor, singer, and dancer in New York, working side gigs in the theatre and as a hairdresser to pay the rent. At times she was broke and worried, but these were very happy times in her life.

Al was also a periodontist and relocated to San Diego to work as an oral surgeon for the VA Medical Center. For most people that's the pinnacle of a successful career, not my Dad. Four years later, in La Jolla, he opened a real estate company called Age of Enlightenment Realty, where many employees were TM meditators. Then, he joined a Petroleum company. Despite jumping from one career to the other, there was always one constant in his life. Teaching TM.

Although Al never taught TM full time, he taught alongside the local San Diego TM teachers and was well-known in the TM community. He had the honor of teaching with the first US appointed TM teacher, Buila Smith, in San Diego.

Laurina thought Al was handsome and charming. She was impressed by how kind, loving, calm, and humble he was. Laurina hadn't met anyone like Al. Matters were complicated with him still being married. He was committed to and supportive of Laurina, and she really felt it was destiny for him to be in her life. Laurina and Al became a couple.

It's hard to know why one's intuition will say something is a big yes, and then later, a big no (they eventually separated), but Laurina says she has no regrets. She felt Al was such an integral part of her spiritual journey. When they were together, she felt loved and heard.

Despite knowing Al only a few months, Laurina flew to California to spend time with him and learn TM. She knew it was going to transform her life and it did.

After that trip, Laurina returned to New York. Summer 1987, Al was traveling back and forth between California to see his family and New York to see Laurina. Once his divorce was finalized, Al moved in with Laurina in Manhattan. Then, tragedy struck. Al's brother Leonard was paralyzed from the neck down from a car accident.

Immediately, Al moved home to Albuquerque to take over his brother's dental practice. A few weeks later, Laurina, now eight months pregnant, joined him. They lived with Al's conservative, Catholic, Spanish parents, Eppie and Alfred, Sr, my grandparents. I was born in Albuquerque on October 28, 1987, the eleventh of fourteen grandchildren. Laurina, then twenty-four, was in labor for four days, and my birth was not easy—which might explain why I am her only child. Once home, Laurina was in baby bliss. She said that she rarely put me down and carried me around like a rag doll.

It's not easy being a new adult in someone's family, but the difficult circumstances of Leonard's accident brought them all together. For a while, Laurina cooked elaborate meals for the family each day. Eppie said it was like a banquet dinner every night. Al and his father, also a dentist, helped keep the dental practice going. Eventually, they moved into a home of their own.

#

New Mexico has a large percentage of Native Americans (11 percent), and a higher percentage of Hispanics (48 percent) than any other state. Native American Pueblo, Spanish, and Anglo are the three major cultural groups of the state. Albuquerque boasts the watermelon pink Sandia Mountains and breathtaking sunsets. The city has a robust spiritual community, including many Native American healers and holistic health practitioners of Traditional Chinese Medicine and Ayurveda. The Ayurveda Institute, founded in 1984 by Dr. Vasant Lad, BAM&S (Bachelor of Ayurvedic Medicine and Surgery), MASc (Master of Ayurvedic Science) is one of many Ayurveda centers in the US.

Dr. Lad was my childhood doctor. At five months old, I got a bad cold and my Western physicians prescribed antibiotics. Laurina said that every time she put the medicine in my mouth, I would spit it out. Laurina's friend recommended Dr. Lad.

Ayurveda, an ancient system of natural medicine, originated in India more than five thousand years ago. The term Ayurveda is derived from the Sanskrit ayur (life) and veda (science or knowledge). Ayurveda translates to knowledge of life—all life. Just as nature has seasons, we humans have biological rhythms. Health and wellness are determined by a delicate balance among the mind, body, and spirit in the moment.

The Ayurvedic way to treat a patient is to discuss symptoms and do pulse assessments. Pulse assessment can determine your dosha, or your mind-body type. The Vaidya or Ayurveda expert will put his fingers on the radial pulse on your wrist. Subtle impulses help to determine the level of ama, or toxins present and/or which organs may need some nourishment or attention. This method can also help to determine which emotions may be out of balance.

After Dr. Lad completes his assessment, he recommends a customized combination of Ayurvedic herbs. These are to be mixed with honey and warm water. Laurina found the herbs, even sweetened with honey were bitter—but I didn't spit them out. I willingly took them. Later, Laurina started learning more about Ayurveda medicine and successfully treated an ear infection I once had by placing warm garlic sesame oil into my ear canal.

Our visits to Dr. Lad's clinic inspired Laurina to immerse herself in learning about Ayurveda. She started to incorporate basic principles into her cooking and daily routine. Soon, it became a complete lifestyle change for our family.

For example, Ayurveda recommends eating the largest meal at noon since the digestive fire is strongest and a lighter meal in the evening. Also, one should include the six tastes: sweet, sour, salty, bitter, pungent, and astringent. If we include all six tastes and favor those tastes best for our dosha, or mind-body type, then we will create more balance in the mind and body. We will feel more satisfied by our meal and may also eat less. Optimal dietary proportions are 50 percent well cooked (not raw) vegetables, 25 percent protein, and 25 percent grain. One can also include a small salad of raw vegetables and lettuce, as well as healthy fats: olive oil, coconut oil, butter, avocado, or ghee (clarified butter).

Ayurveda believes that for maximum nutrient absorption, food ideally should be eaten right after it's prepared. Even leftovers are better if homemade. Laurina continued to cook family meals daily, but now she used only fresh ingredients. Al was on board. I, of course, had no choice since I was a baby. Laurina would steam veggies and put them through a blender or sieve to make my baby food. As I got older, I naturally ate the way she did and unlike many kids, I loved vegetables and still do.

#

In 1993, when I was five years old, my parents separated. My mom wanted to find herself and felt called to go to Europe. Laurina and I moved to a small town in northwest Germany, Schledehausen. Population 1000. Schledehausen was an important TM community in Europe, with a large number of TM teachers and meditators living and working there. The TM headquarters and a world class Maharishi Ayurveda spa in Schledehausen provided jobs and community. Although English was my first language, I learned German pretty quickly once we moved there. I don't even remember learning; I just suddenly spoke and wrote it.

Schledehausen was less culturally diverse than neighboring Osnabrück. It had very little cultural diversity. I was the exotic Native American, Spanish, and Italian descendant. My German helped me fit in. Once I went to school in Osnabrück, where all the middle school kids went after they completed sixth grade in the smaller towns, I started to feel less like an outsider. And yet, when I later returned to America—to Fairfield, Iowa—I was an outsider from Germany. I couldn't win.

I would return to America most summers for six weeks, the first half in New York and New Jersey, to be with Laurina's parents, Trudy and Nat Buro, and the second half in New Mexico, with Al and his parents, Eppie and Alfred, Sr. I have wonderful memories of all my grandparents. Both sets of grandparents would take me back-to-school shopping, and I would return to Germany each fall with stylish American clothes.

In New York and New Jersey, Trudy and my aunts and uncles would sometimes serve me cheese pizza and even, once, a McDonald's cheeseburger. Laurina wasn't thrilled. Trudy used to make a Greek pasta salad with lots of veggies, which I often still make today. Grandpa Lopez had a whole freezer of Häagen-Dazs ice cream that we would eat at night while watching TV.

#

My upbringing was unconventional—to say the least. Laurina is one of the most fanatical health nuts of all time, and was and still is like a drill sergeant when it comes to healthy eating. She was a vegetarian and so, neither cooked nor served meat in our house. Candy and other interesting sweets were nowhere to be found. Laurina and I were eating all organic whole grain before it was a thing. The guy from the Reformhaus (natural co-op or grocery) would deliver boxes and boxes of healthy food weekly, including whole grain, freshly baked bread.

Everyone likely has a moment where they look at their peers' family life and think maybe they have it better. You may be envious if your friends or siblings have greater intelligence, wealth, fame, or are better looking. Every young person has to grapple with comparing oneself to others. As adults, we realize that it does not serve us well.

Throughout my childhood in Germany, I remember going to other people's houses and thinking things appeared more normal. First, only a few of my classmates had parents who meditated and most of my classmates had married parents or if divorced, had more involved fathers. Most of my other TM friends were a grade above me at the same school. Second, most of my classmates' food was from the average local grocery store.

Because there was no junk food in our house—only carob (carob doesn't taste exactly like chocolate, but it has a nutty flavor, and carob powder and carob chips can be substituted one-for-one for cocoa powder and chocolate chips in recipes)—I had to get my fix somewhere. When I would go to my friends' house, I would eat almost everything they offered me. Chips. Chocolate. Candy. I sure enjoyed it, even if my taste buds didn't know what to make of the new flavors of salty chips and sugary candy.

Eventually, I started eating at school more and buying the breakfast roll with butter and cheese on it. My love for bread and cheese developed in Germany. It's been hard to cut bread and cheese out of my diet, because it's so delicious. However, it doesn't always love me back sometimes causing lethargy and congestion. Everything in moderation, right?

I was fascinated by how neat my classmates' white, store-bought processed bread sandwiches looked. My sandwich bread, which we sliced ourselves for optimal freshness, sometimes fell apart. My classmates made fun of me for having sloppy bread and being a vegetarian. Fortunately, there was one other vegetarian in the class.

Small differences between me and my classmates began to chip away at my self-esteem. Moments of ridicule big and small weighed heavily on my young heart. Now I can laugh about it and feel grateful that Laurina fed me the cleanest possible food, but I felt so different then. Maybe it wasn't the different food or the meditation. Maybe I would've felt this way had I stayed in the States. Maybe I would have felt insecure about something else. But then, it was all about our lifestyle and being foreigners in a time like the 90's.

#

When I was nine years old, fall 1997, Laurina went to Seelisberg, Switzerland, for five months to become a TM teacher. I stayed behind in Germany. I was excited for her to fulfill a dream of hers. Even though I was young to be apart from my mother, I understood this was something she wanted and needed to do. A local TM family, the Hermands, offered to let me live with them. Their daughter Saraswati was a year ahead of me at the local school, although we did not know each other well. Saraswati had two other siblings, also with Sanskrit names.

I had not lived near extended family since we left Albuquerque four years before. I was being raised by a single mom, and once we moved to Germany, I saw my dad only once a year in the summer. I wanted to be part of a large family again. Living with the Hermands was different, but easy. We practiced TM as a family, but sometimes the parents would send us kids upstairs to practice our word of wisdom and we'd just goof off. Most of the time, though, I took it very seriously. My German even improved. Saraswati and I had our challenges at first (her parents gave me a lot of attention), but then we became best friends and are still in touch.

In Germany, the summer break is typically shorter than in the US, and every fall, we would get a two-week break. Most German families went to Spain, Turkey, Italy, or Greece for their vacations. On my tenth birthday, in 1997, over the fall break, the Hermands and I went to Mallorca, Spain. I loved being by the ocean. Saraswati and I swam a lot and buried each other in the sand. We had pastries, fresh fruit, and juice for breakfast, and took long walks on the beach. Given my Spanish features, I felt more at home in Spain than I had in Germany.

At ten, children can learn the adult TM technique. I could have learned from Saraswati's parents, Jost and Eleanore, who were TM teachers, but I wanted to wait and learn from Laurina.

Before an instructor teaches a student TM and on special occasions like a birthday, they perform a ceremony of gratitude. Jost fulfilled this tradition for me on my tenth birthday. I wore one of my favorite dresses, and felt blissful. Watching Jost hold the flowers and move his hands with the song of gratitude was fascinating. I somehow knew that I wanted to be able to perform this for others one day.

After the vacation, back in Germany, I had a few more months of school. I celebrated Christmas with the Hermands, and then Laurina came back from Switzerland around New Year's Eve. It was a cold winter night. Laurina snuck into my bed and cuddled me and held me tightly. I could feel her excitement of having become a TM teacher, but also having her little girl back by her side. I had missed her a lot, too, but the time somehow went by quickly.

Then on January 4, 1998, Laurina taught me the adult TM

technique. I was her first student. Somehow, I don't remember this day. TM teaches you how to transcend, which means to go beyond the surface of the mind to the quieter levels of thinking. I was probably so excited and transcended right away. Everyone transcends when they first learn to meditate. Some remember it clearly, some don't—regardless of age. I knew my experience was something special, especially because I learned from my mother right after her TM Teaching Training course.

The following week, Laurina and I went to see Maharishi Mahesh Yogi, who lived in Vlodrop, Netherlands. Vlodrop is a town in the southeastern part of the Netherlands near the German border. Vlodrop was a separate municipality until 1991, when it merged with Melick en Herkenbosch.

Vlodrop was the site of the European headquarters for TM. Maharishi may have chosen to live there to have a quiet place to work. His house is situated in the woods and very peaceful. He may have also felt it was an easy hub, between the States and India, for international activities. Maharishi was getting older and not traveling as much, but did like to have larger conferences in Vlodrop, where meditators and TM teachers would gather. He always said that Holland was a peaceful country.

It was tradition for Maharishi to meet by videoconference

(and starting with classes of December 1997, by phone) with the latest TM Teacher Training Course (TTC) graduates internationally the week after their ceremony.

We didn't meet him in person, but we did go into the house where Maharishi lived, took his work calls, and met with his staff. We sat quietly, waiting to speak to him through conference call.

When we were on the phone with him in another building, Laurina was the only one who had the courage to say: "Maharishi, we made these flower garlands for you." And then, he said something like: "OK, come on over then." I was excited and knew how special it was for him to invite us all into his home.

We were welcomed into a living room area. Maharishi remained upstairs, but called down by phone to continue meeting with the group. I don't recall what else he said or was discussed. It was an honor to have been in his presence—the closest I came to meeting him personally. I am so grateful.

#

In Germany, when I was a teenager, Laurina ran the TM center out of our small, two-bedroom apartment. Some of the houses and apartments there had kitchens and living rooms with doors for privacy. I was able to be in my room while Laurina worked. We had one lovely apartment with high ceilings that had been the mayor's house decades before. It was right in the center of town.

Not all TM centers are run out of private homes, although many are, especially in smaller towns. Since TM is a nonprofit organization and meditators have free lifetime follow-up with an instructor, it's not always financially feasible to have a separate office.

All the TM teaching and related events for that area were happening in our living room. Fortunately, it wasn't like Grand Central Station, with people in and out all the time. As an only child, I still had Laurina's full attention and I always felt like her priority. Of course, when friends came over, I still sometimes resented the optics—the scent of incense, candles, and photos of Maharishi and his teacher, Guru Dev—that I was basically living at a TM center. The photos probably didn't stand out to my friends as much as I thought they did.

In hindsight, I probably worried more than I needed to. I was popular then and had some good friends. It's not that they abandoned me because of Laurina's profession, but it was unusual and another way I was different from my peers.

I wanted to be like everyone else. For a short time, I gave up regular TM practice in Germany. TM had brought me so much relief from stress and anxiety and allowed me to experience my own inner peace. I gave it up when I needed it most. I might have gotten through my struggle with schoolwork in Germany had I been doing TM twice a day. I may have rebelled to show I was my own person. In retrospect, I was trying to fit in with my peers. It was not a good decision. What we need most may be right in front of us. We can't always see it or be ready to receive it.

I believe that our decisions are sometimes rooted in a deeper purpose. Maybe I had to stop meditating and suffer for a while to learn the value of TM practice. Maybe if everything had been going along fine in Germany, I would not have encouraged Laurina to leave and return to America—which we soon did.

#

Growing up with TM and Ayurveda taught me my first life lesson: discipline is a practice. Laurina reinforced the habit. Being disciplined has supported my robust health.

Knock on wood, I've never been to the hospital and have rarely had to go to urgent care. I've basically lived my entire life without using over-the-counter and prescription medications; however, my natural medicine chest is overrun with vitamins and natural supplements. It's a monumental feat in today's world, given so much toxicity from the use of pesticides, polluted oceans and air, EMF exposure, and more. My preference is to seek more natural ways to heal, but I value modern medicine and would take it if needed. My goal is to stay so healthy that I do not need it.

The mind and body are intimately connected. Whatever we do to the mind effects the body, and vice versa. This is why the TM technique is the first line of defense to develop one's consciousness as a means to better health. By practicing TM regularly, we are enlivening the body's inner intelligence to maintain good health.

Here are my tips to help you develop discipline to promote health and well-being and anything else you wish to achieve.

Tips for Lesson 1: Discipline Is a Practice

1. Take stock of your health

    If you are not in good physical or mental health for some reason, focus on that first. The healthier you are, the easier it will be to have the desire and energy to be disciplined.

2. Start small and with small routines

Remember the expression "Rome wasn't built in a day." Just make one tiny change at a time. For example, by establishing a more regular wakeup, bedtime, or eating time, you will help your body and mind know what to do when. Then, keep doing it. Make the small step a small routine, and you will be more likely to succeed in your new and better habits.

3. Balance your needs

Be aware of where you are and what you need in the present moment. Prioritize what is most important. This may mean you need to reduce—or even stop—activities that don't bring you joy, disrupt your routine, waste your time, or zap your energy.

4. Get off the hamster wheel

Start and end your day with the Transcendental Meditation technique. Morning meditation sets a more peaceful tone for the day and allows you to be more mindful and focused. Early evening meditation releases accumulated tension from the day, boosts your energy, and helps you sleep better at night. TM allows your mind to settle down, and it will be easier for you to maintain a good daily routine.

5. Prioritize urgent tasks and set reminders

Not everyone has a highly structured job with a built-in routine, or works well under pressure with looming deadlines. Discipline should release, not increase, tension. Differentiate between what is urgent and what is important. Keep track of your goals and the step-by-step tasks necessary to reach them. Mark up your calendar with reminders of what to do when. You will feel a sense of accomplishment as you complete each task and will be less likely to stray from your priorities. If unforeseen circumstances arise, be gentle with yourself and begin again.

6. Make an appointment for self-care

Just like in the workplace, in our personal life, we can prioritize and schedule our healthy routines (and reminders) to eat well, exercise, and do other self-care. Plan your meals in advance and bring snacks with you on the go. Set a regular walking date with a friend. Pre-book a series of body treatments, such as massage, acupuncture, red light therapy, salt booth, etc. Advance preparation and standing appointments make it easier to stay mindful—and say "no, thank you" when your colleague brings you that donut.

7. Avoid rigidity

Being overly strict will add to stress and worry and may undermine your success. Favor flexibility. Embrace balance. Discipline can be comfortable—even fun. For instance, build in a cheat day or a cheat meal. Reward your successes along the way.

8. Honor your natural ways

Some people are, by nature, morning people; others are night owls. Some people move quickly and others, more slowly. We all have different ways of being in the world. We are not meant to be the same. Try not to be so hard on yourself if your rhythm is not yet where you want it to be or is out of sync with others' patterns. Be authentic. Be you.

Notice how much better you are starting to feel as your new discipline becomes routine. Remember, change takes time. Celebrate your wins along the way.

LESSON 2
Find Your Community

Moving to Fairfield, Iowa

You will come across many people in your life. They will all have a purpose to fulfil. Some will teach you a lesson and some will leave your soul wounded. Some will love you for their selfish motives and some will love you unconditionally. Some will cheat you, lie to you and stab you in the back. Learn from the lessons life teaches you and don't waste your time on people who are there in your life for their convenience and who never take you seriously. Don't allow people to use you for their selfish reasons. Just be strong and don't let anything break you or leave you shattered. Choose the people whom you want in your life.

Aarti Khurana

Try something new, attract your community and experience a sense of belonging.

After a whirlwind ten years abroad, in 2003, Laurina asked me if I was ready to move back to the States. If we stayed in Germany, I might have had to repeat ninth grade. Studying three languages—German, English, and French—was intensely demanding and I was doing poorly in a few other subjects, too. I needed enough As and Bs to balance out the Ds. So, I was ready to come back to America. At first, we were going to visit before we moved, but then I told Laurina I didn't need to visit. Let's just move. My intuition confirmed it was the right choice.

Laurina and I finally landed at Eastern Iowa Airport in Cedar Rapids and were in a car on our way to Fairfield. We wanted to move back so we could each study at consciousness-based schools (Laurina wanted to finish her college education).

A consciousness-based school was one where the focus was on the development of consciousness itself, not just a focus on different fields of study. In Fairfield, both the high school (Maharishi School) and university (Maharishi International University) apply a consciousness-based education. The system of education was not just to fill the consciousness (the container of knowledge) with more facts, but was to expand the container of knowledge itself, so that it could absorb more knowledge.

Fairfield is home to the Maharishi International University (MIU) campus, where all the TM educational and training campuses are located, including a K–12 private school; the Global Mother Divine Organization (GMDO) for Women (this is a wing of the TM organization that focuses on women learning TM); the US headquarters for the TM organization; and the Raj Health Spa, an ayurvedic health center.

Laurina and I arrived on a cold, snowy January day, but the sun shone brightly. Germany was cold and gloomy most of the year. We were lucky if any summer day reached seventy degrees.

The closer we got to Fairfield, the more excited I was to start a new life where I felt I might belong and not be bullied by my classmates. Even my close friends in Germany had teased me.

The admissions counselor at the Maharishi School picked

us up from the airport and drove us to the MIU campus. The town felt so peaceful under the bright sun. I had been to Fairfield once before, as a toddler when Laurina took a TM Advanced Technique course. My memories are vague, but the nourishing feeling of warmth and security never left me. I felt it once again.

Laurina and I stayed in a dorm on the college campus until we found permanent housing. On my first day of middle school, I was introduced to a lot of people and heard whispering in the hallways. I was later told they were saying: "That is the new German girl." Even though I am not German, having come from there, I was the new German girl. I was coming from a small city in Germany, only slightly larger than this small rural town of almost ten thousand people.

I was wearing a chic, beige down coat and beige faux leather stiletto boots—not what teen girls were wearing there. One of the seniors told me years later that they thought I was a "news reporter with good style." Fairfield had been in the news before (Oprah Winfrey called it one of America's most unusual towns ("America's Most Unusual Town", Oprah's Next Chapter, April 8, 2011)), so it was normal for reporters and film crews to be at the school. Another friend told me recently that some of the guys had a crush on me.

I was there to study and glad to trade in my fashionable wardrobe for the school uniform: a white blouse with a khaki skort, and in winter, a yellow sweater. Loafers, too, and mine had to be cute. I still tried to dress up my uniform as any fifteen-year-old would, but was relieved not to have to figure out what to wear every day. I would wear longer earrings than I should have, and sometimes hike up my skort if I saw my high school crush. I wore a little makeup, but less than I had in Germany. My '70s blue eye shadow, which had made a comeback in the '90s, would not have flown in Fairfield.

Everyone in my consciousness-based school practiced Transcendental Meditation, twice daily as a group in the morning before school and in the afternoon before physical education class. Every school subject in our curriculum was connected to consciousness, in the sense that each subject at its most fundamental level had an underlying foundation that was closely connected to the fundamental principles of consciousness. I noticed a huge difference from my German public school. Classes were separated by gender, which I was happy about, but we shared the building. My new teachers were friendly and nice, and everyone had this ease and glow about them. Although my class of twenty-five girls had its cliques, they were welcoming. I think one of the reasons the other students were more accepting was due to the fact that everyone was practicing TM. TM helps to reduce stress and naturally makes the heart more refined, so that people tend to be more harmonious with others spontaneously.

Therefore, I felt much more at home than I had in school abroad. I was still fairly reserved and shy, but soon became more comfortable and learned to trust my friends and classmates.

My routine and lifestyle were changing quickly, but it felt natural. When I arrived at school in the mornings, I first went to the meditation hall, called the "hall of bliss," where students meditated together. We also practiced yoga and breathing techniques, which I was already familiar with. I learned to read and speak Sanskrit, an ancient language of India. Every morning before class, we read Sanskrit in unison. During breakfast, I studied this new language and its alphabet. Within a month, I was able to slowly read with the group and eventually, with practice, could recite it fast.

Reading Sanskrit increases brain wave coherence, an optimal way to start your day. According to Dr. Fred Travis, a brain researcher, who is the Director of the Center for Brain, Consciousness, & Cognition at Maharishi International University, "The Transcendental Meditation technique locates pure consciousness, leading to the state of Transcendental Consciousness, reading Sanskrit integrates inner silence with outer activity, helping to cultivate enlightenment." ("Reading Sanskrit Improves Brain Functioning", Brynne Sissom, *MUM Review* (6 February 2002)).

#

My favorite part of our new life was group meditation with my classmates. Although I had strong support at home and with some of my friends in Germany, group meditation was a different experience. The benefits I experienced from meditating regularly were calm energy, confidence, inner happiness, and feeling a lot less overwhelmed.

In Fairfield, there is another dimension to community, which really goes to a whole new level of understanding of what community is. Maharishi started talking about collective consciousness way back in the '70s as more and more Americans were learning the TM technique. He predicted that, if individuals started experiencing greater harmony and happiness within themselves through the practice of the TM technique, this harmony and happiness would start to spread throughout the surrounding community, even to non-meditating individuals.

Fairfield, Iowa became the center for research into this phenomenon of how individuals can affect and transform the society around them through the practice of the TM program. This phenomenon became known over time as the "Maharishi Effect".

One of the earliest examples of this phenomenon took place back in 1978, when there were several countries that were experiencing violence from war in their country. Maharishi heard that the citizens from one of these countries were asking if anyone could help them to end the violence of a civil war happening in their country. Maharishi responded by sending a group of about 1400 individuals trained in the TM program and a more advanced program, called the TM-Sidhi program, to these five countries (Nicaragua,

Lebanon, Zimbabwe, Iran, and Thailand). The group of 1400 was divided up into smaller groups for each country.

These individuals were sent to stay in hotels in those countries at a safe distance from the violence in the country. In those hotels, these groups practiced the TM and TM-Sidhi techniques together twice a day. Maharishi predicted that this would alleviate the violence in the countries, even though the individuals were not directly interacting with anyone in the country. The effect they were creating was purely on the level of consciousness, where they were creating harmony and coherence within their own awareness, and this effect of harmony was then spreading out to the consciousness of the citizens of the country.

The results of this experiment were fascinating. Later, when research was done on this 1978 experiment, it was shown that hostile actions in the countries decreased by 36% compared to the time before the groups assembled.

This confirmed the theory that introducing a small group of meditating individuals into the collective consciousness of a country was able to reduce violence in the country. In one example, Zimbabwe, the deaths per day dropped by 81% when the group was in the country.

(Study: Orme-Johnson, D. W., Dillbeck, M. C., Bousquet, J. G., & Alexander, C. N. (1989). An experimental analysis of the application of the Maharishi Technology of the Unified Field in major world trouble spots. In: R. A, Chalmers, G. Clements, H. Schenkluhn, & M. Weinless (Eds.), *Scientific research on Maharishi's Transcendental Meditation and TM-Sidhi programme: Collected papers, volume 4*, (pp. 2532-2548). The Netherlands: Maharishi Vedic University Press.)

A few years later, in 1983, a similar study was done in Israel, where a group of about 200 TM Program practitioners assembled in Israel to try to influence a war conflict in the neighboring country of Lebanon. In the thirteen days before the meditating group was at its peak, the average number of deaths per day was 33.7. During the thirteen days with the peak number of meditators assembled together, the average number of deaths per day was 1.5 per day. In the thirteen days after the peak number of meditators, the average number of deaths per day went back up to thirty-three deaths per day. In other words, the number of people dying during this war dropped dramatically when this group of TM practitioners assembled, and then the number of deaths rose dramatically after the group departed.

(Study: Orme-Johnson, D. W., Alexander, C. N., Davies, J. L., Chandler, H. M., & Larimore, W. E. (1988). International peace project in the Middle East: The effect of the Maharishi Technology of the Unified Field. *Journal of Conflict Resolution, 32*(4), 776-812.)

Since that time, there have now been about fifty studies done on this same phenomenon, with some of those studies involving very large groups of individuals. It has been found over and over that quality of life improves in many different ways from the presence of these "coherence-creating" meditating groups. Some of the examples are: reduction in murder rates, reduction in number of deaths, reduction in crime, reduced hospital admissions, increased peace, improved economic activity, and an increased feeling of positivity. There are more details of these findings in the following paper: (Orme-Johnson, D. W., & Fergusson, L. (2018). Global impact of the Maharishi Effect from 1974 to 2017: Theory and research. *Journal of Maharishi Vedic Research Institute*, *8*, 13-79)

All of these findings reinforce the idea that we are very connected to our community, and can profoundly transform our community in a positive way, when we increase the harmony and coherence in our own life through the TM program and TM-Sidhi program, and when we are able to practice these techniques in groups.

Another healthy addition to my routine was eating at the cafeteria, hosted by the university. The classes sat together mostly, but all grades ate there, and I would sometimes have lunch with Laurina. My daily, nutrient dense meals helped focus my mind and strengthen my body tremendously. It was also a welcome break for Laurina to have prepared, organic vegetarian food rather than needing to cook during the week.

Schoolwork and studying hadn't always come easily to me, but now, it finally did. I still wasn't one of the gifted, brilliant students who had been at the school most of their lives, but it was much easier for me to want to listen to my teachers, study, and learn. I could finally keep up with the pace and school workload—or at least was less shy to ask for help. I joined track and cross-country. Although I wasn't good at the other sports like volleyball and basketball, I loved to run, and I became fit.

Outside of school and on weekends, I was pretty social. For a small town, Fairfield had many cultural offerings, such as the First Fridays Art Walk and theatre productions. My friends and I would often meet at one of the local restaurants or coffee shops for dinner, watch movies on the weekend, and of course, have a shopping spree here and there.

We fundraised for our senior trip to the Virgin Islands by selling calendars, illustrated with our artwork and photography for each month. One of my artworks made it onto the cover. For someone to whom art doesn't come easily, I was proud. Going door-to-door at our condo complex to sell the senior calendar, I happened to knock on the door of my dad's TM teacher when he learned TM in Kansas City in 1972.

I said something like: "Hello, my name is Olivia Lopez. I am a senior at the Maharishi School. Would you like to buy a calendar?"

The gentleman said, "Yes, I'd like to buy one. Are you, by chance, related to Al Lopez?"

I said, "Yes. He's my dad!"

He said, "Wow. I am his TM teacher."

The way my dad had always talked about Maharishi, I thought that Maharishi was his TM teacher. But then, I met the person who really taught my dad TM.

\#

In 2007, after fourteen years of being a single mom, Laurina married Bolton Carroll and moved to Chicago. They were introduced through a mutual friend, Susan, who is like a godmother and mentor to me. Laurina was in Chicago to consult with a biological dentist who removes mercury fillings. Laurina and Bolton met for dinner and hit it off right away. The waitress said it seemed like the two had known each other a long time. They have been happily married now for fifteen years.

Although Laurina had longed to get married again, she hadn't found the right one. Her experience taught me patience. Sometimes timing is everything, and we just have to wait until the universe decides when the time is right. If we look deeper, we can often find the purpose and meaning of the delay.

February 4, 2008, Maharishi Mahesh Yogi passed away. It was a very sad time for those in the TM organization since Maharishi was a source of deep knowledge for us all. For sixty years, he had been available to his followers and accessible to the media. He had held weekly press conferences between 2002 and 2007, and was interviewed by Larry King (May 12, 2002) and others. To his followers, Maharishi always inspired us by helping us on the path toward higher states of consciousness.

Laurina and Bolton decided to travel to India for Maharishi's funeral. They asked me if I would like to join them. For this world traveler, my answer was an immediate yes! Although Bolton had been to India before, it would be Laurina's and my first time. It was a lot to plan. We would fly into Delhi, and then travel by car to Allahabad, the location of the funeral and Maharishi's ashram.

OLIVIA LOPEZ

You had to be a true devotee, given the meager lodgings and minimal comforts in Allahabad. As Americans, we are quite spoiled to have such a high standard of living throughout our country, compared to residents of India in some parts of their country. Since Allahabad was a smaller town and so many people wanted to go to the funeral, the better hotels were sold out. An estimated twenty thousand people passed through to pay their respects ("Thousands Throng Allahabad for Mahesh Yogi's Funeral", Daijiworld.com, February 11, 2008, https://daijiworld.com/index.php/news/newsDisplay?newsID=43389).

When we arrived and checked out the available hotels, we were pretty shocked. Some did not even have a shower or running hot water. You either took a cold shower or they would bring you a bucket with warm water in the morning. There was also no heat, and it got cold at night. Don't even think about having breakfast. They would serve a dosa, which is a thin pancake with a variety of fillings, such as veggies, rice, and lentils. It may sound delicious, but they always use extremely hot spices that would burn your mouth and would also quite often send you to the bathroom. I guess I didn't have it in me, at twenty years old, to endure limited amenities. At some point, I broke down and said to Laurina, "All I want is a hot bath and a hot cup of tea."

For a few days, they had a viewing of Maharishi before the cremation that would take place outside. There were long lines to get into the room. Anyone who was coming from outside of India had priority to go in first. We were packed in the place like sardines, and it was hard to move about without bumping into people. On the morning of the cremation, we were waiting in the ashram totally in awe of the number of people that continued to arrive to pay respect to Maharishi, such as the Indian Army, David Lynch, and other famous people.

Then the moment came to bring the body close to the Ganges River. It is customary that only men walk in the procession and the women watch on TV. Laurina and I watched on TV with thousands of people cramming to get into the large room where we were, while my stepdad joined the procession walking down to the river. Thousands of followers waved flags, beat drums, clanged cymbals, and chanted hymns. They carried the flower-covered body from the Maharishi's ashram to a hilltop overlooking the confluence of the sacred Ganges and Yamuna rivers. It is a Vedic tradition to cremate the body and then spread the ashes in multiple locations. Although we stayed about a week, it was not enough time to complete the entire pilgrimage of spreading Maharishi's ashes in multiple locations.

After Allahabad, we went to Varanasi, where we stayed at a beautiful, modern hotel with great food and plenty of hot running water. Allahabad and Varanasi are two of the holiest cities in all of India. Allahabad is considered a very spiritual location, since it sits at the confluence of three sacred rivers. Varanasi is one of the oldest cities in the world, and is considered by many to be the holiest city in India. Both cities are on the banks of the Ganges River, and in both Allhabad and Varanasi, I dipped in the holy water of the Ganges. One of my best friends from school in Fairfield was also in India for the funeral, and made it onto the cover of an Indian newspaper.

It was a humbling experience to be in India. I realized how lucky I am, in the West, to have basic conveniences like running water, hot water, and toilets. However, in India, regardless of their caste or class and with few material possessions, the people are very happy. I gained perspective about what we truly need: food, love, and shelter. Anything else is just a bonus.

#

After middle school and high school, I earned my BA and MBA from Maharishi International University and went on to become a TM teacher in 2010. I ended up living in Fairfield for over ten years, between 2003 and 2014. I left occasionally between 2010 and 2013 for a few work trips to California, but didn't leave permanently until April 2014. I still go back every summer to see my friends, and also to attend the annual TM Teacher Conference.

Moving to Fairfield was the best decision that Laurina and I made. It truly helped me become who I am today. I will always be grateful for my time there and it will always have a special place in my heart.

Finding community is vital to our mental well-being. Research shows that having a supportive community lowers anxiety, lifts depression, and eases loneliness. Other benefits are higher self-esteem, more empathy, and greater trust of others. I experienced all of these benefits living in Fairfield, and after a decade there, it was hard to leave. Since that time, I have found community wherever I lived, but I have also had times of isolation.

Here are my tips to help you find a community of like-minded people and become an engaged and helpful community member.

Tips for Lesson 2: Find Your Community

1. Try something new

    Every time you leave your comfort zone, you grow a little bit. Something good will usually come out of it, including meeting new people with a shared goal or interest. Go someplace in your area you've never been to. Take a different route to work and notice the landscape. Try something you thought you'd never do. I like trying new things, whether it's a new workout class, a café, or traveling somewhere I've never been. By trying something new, you are stimulating your appetite for new experiences.

2. Join the crowd

    Find and meet, online or in person, like-minded people or groups with shared interests. Attend a workshop. Take a class. Join a gym. Sign up for a book club. Host a Zoom social event like game night. If you are a TM Practitioner, go on a TM retreat, which are offered across the country and online several times each month (https://www.tmretreats.org/home). They usually last a half-day, a day, or a weekend.

3. Attend networking events.

As an adult, in every new city I moved to, I attended business networking events. Sometimes I went all by myself. I would give my sixty-second introduction to the fifty or so people in the room and feel shy. But it always gave me confidence and I usually left with at least one contact that turned into a friendship.

4. Honor your inner homebody

Even extroverts can feel lonely and need community. Introverts and in particular, empaths (highly sensitive individuals who have a keen ability to sense what people around them are thinking and feeling) need to monitor how much stimulation is useful. Sometimes, introverts need to be adopted by the right extrovert and just join in. Sometimes, introverts feel a sense of belonging by just being a good neighbor and a good citizen. Aim for brief interactions that are sincere, helpful, kind, and pleasant.

5. Accept others

Finding your community also means being a good community member. Having been bullied as a child, I aim to always be inclusive and especially welcoming to the newcomer. Newcomers can also teach us how to become more independent and resilient. Love your family and friends where they are and know you can't change anyone. You can only change how you interact with others. Sometimes that means setting proper boundaries, expressing any hurt feelings, and standing up for yourself and how you deserve to be treated.

6. Be supportive

We can help build community through supportive action, such as shopping local, volunteering, and checking in with our neighbors. Just listening, being empathetic, and offering words of compassion can be very helpful to others. By helping others, by giving back, you strengthen the collective and your ties to it.

Think broadly about what community means to you. In Fairfield, I was with fellow meditators, and felt at home. Later, as an adult opening TM centers in unfamiliar cities, I had to learn to honor my introversion while building communities of meditators. Most of all, reaching outside of yourself by helping others (for me, now, that's through teaching and coaching) is my best advice to connect with others and find community.

LESSON 3
With Focus, Anything Is Possible

Becoming a TM Teacher

> *The happiest people don't have the best of everything, they just make the best of everything.*
>
> Anonymous

Through well-being regimens, taking care of your health, and directed goals, you can increase your ability to focus.

August 2009, I was in my first semester of MBA classes at MIU, and I received an email that the TM Teacher Training Course (TTC) had been postponed from September to October. My half-sister was getting married early October and because I was living in Germany when some of my other half-siblings married, I was determined to attend this one.

Al's next-youngest is ten years older than I am; his eldest is a few years younger than Laurina. I didn't grow up with them since they were born and raised in San Diego (and still live there). They did visit us in New Mexico during summers and some holidays when I was a toddler before I moved to Germany. In 2003 when I moved back to the US, Al flew me to San Diego from New Mexico so we could get reacquainted. That was a great trip.

When I received the email advertising the Teacher Training Course, I had a strong intuition to apply. Laurina was pleasantly surprised by my plan. She had always encouraged me to become a TM teacher, but never pressured me. She knew that if it's not my idea, I can be pretty stubborn.

I knew I wanted to become a TM teacher someday, but planned to first become a fashion designer (it's still a dream of mine) or a business owner. Helping people has always been a passion of mine. My friends will tell you I always give insightful advice and am a great listener (too great sometimes and will let extroverts or ramblers ramble on), and always have ideas and creative solutions for people's problems and personal struggles.

My intuition told me that now was the time to go for training. I couldn't ignore the feeling. I applied, was accepted within a few weeks, and went to my half sister's wedding in San Diego. Then, I came back to Fairfield to pack up my dorm room and go to my five-month, in-residence TM Teacher Training Course in the Iowa countryside. I was able to pause my graduate studies to take the course and even received some course credit.

Arriving at the teacher training campus on the TM for Women Campus in Vedic City, I had the same feelings as I had when I arrived in Fairfield six years before. Excited. A sense of belonging. Being at peace. Vedic City is about fifteen minutes north of Fairfield and is its own town with its own mayor. The Iowa countryside is even more rural than the university campus only five miles away.

Eight ladies were on my course, and we became a very tight-knit group. In the TTC, genders are separated; however, back in the '70s, some activities were mixed and many TM couples met and lots of TM babies were born. Courses were gender segregated now to minimize distractions and maximize focus.

During the TTC, everything is done to limit disruptions, including the rural setting and prepared meals. Students do not leave campus for the duration of the program. I learned then how beneficial TM is to my ability to focus—even though the technique does not require focus.

From my training on the TM technique, I learned some of the basic points about TM. Here are some of the essential lessons I learned.

> I and other TM practitioners love the effortless transcending that happens with TM. The mind takes a dive into the transcendent in the most natural way. The transcendent is a silent level within our mind, which is beyond the surface level of our thinking process, and which is the source of all of our creativity, intelligence, and energy. Most people experience the transcendent as deep inner silence, peacefulness, and bliss.

Most other forms of meditation use focus or concentration, such as following the breath or concentrating on some thought, which keeps the mind on the surface level. This can cause strain and even anxiety as one tries to hold onto a thought or push away unintended thoughts. Although TM is mantra-based, the mantra is a vehicle to the quieter level—without requiring focus. You enter a state of consciousness called Transcendental Consciousness, and the technique is known as "effortless transcendence." You have to learn TM and experience its ease to truly understand what that means.

Here's an analogy. Think of your mind like a giant ocean. At the surface the waves are active and can be rough, but as soon as you take a dive and go to the bottom of the ocean, it gets quieter. If you have ever snorkeled or scuba dived, or seen it in a movie, you know how beautiful and quiet the depths are. However, it's also still active with many species and plant life. It is really its own universe.

That's how our mind works. When it's quiet, the answers usually come. But not when we are stressed and in fight, flight, or freeze mode. Only when the body and mind are in balance can we experience our true authentic self.

In TM, we transcend, or go beyond the surface of the mind, to where everything our mind has learned and experienced is. When we tap into this, our subconscious mind, we can experience our true desires and succeed.

When you've had a goal and a desire, wouldn't you say sometimes it just shows up without you trying? Well, that's called "flow." Or, experiencing the transcendence during an activity.

When our brains become more orderly and coherent by resting, we can strengthen existing pathways, change bad habits, cope with addiction, and restore our brains to have a "super mind". That's what TM can offer you.

#

The TM technique is practiced while sitting comfortably in a chair with the eyes closed. It's enjoyable and can be easily learned by anyone at any age. The benefits are immediate and increase over time. You feel calmer and more focused throughout the day.

TM has always been and still is taught in seven steps, which are outlined below. The initial instruction (step 4 below) is always one-on-one and in person, and the three follow-up sessions (steps 5–7 below) are either in person or via Zoom.

Step 1: Attend TM Intro talk, in person or online.

The first lecture gives a vision of possibilities for personal development through the Transcendental Meditation Program. This informational session can be done either in person or by phone.

Topics covered include:

A few of the seven hundred scientific research studies showing the benefits to one's health.

The impact of stress on our health and how TM can help by reducing cortisol, the stress hormone.

TM is not a religion, philosophy, or way of life. It is a technique to manage stress; however, it does come from India and was founded by Maharishi Mahesh Yogi (1918–2008).

Attendees interested in learning TM complete a questionnaire, have a brief individual interview with the teacher, and schedule personal instruction.

Step 2: Attend a second lecture.

This group lecture explains more about the mechanics, uniqueness, and origin of the Transcendental Meditation technique. This is usually done via Zoom, the online video conferencing platform, once someone decides to learn the TM technique.

Step 3: Have a private interview.

In the private interview, the teacher becomes acquainted with the person about to start the Transcendental Meditation technique. This can be done any time before the first day of instruction, or even on the day of instruction itself.

Steps 4–7: Step 4: Learn the TM technique.

Receiving instructions of the actual practice itself is always done on four consecutive days, for about one hour each day.

On the first day, the student sits with the teacher for private, individual instruction.

Steps 5–7: Attend three group verification and validation follow-ups, in person or online, on three consecutive days.

In person follow-ups are sixty to ninety minutes, depending on class size and how many questions people ask. In each follow-up, the student learns what their personal experiences during meditation mean, and the student learns the mechanics of the easy and natural process of transcending.

There is also a digital option to receive the follow-up content in an interactive online course. It is taught by Maharishi's successor Tony Nader, MD, PhD and includes clips from Maharishi's videos. Essentially, the student is learning the details and nuances of the technique directly from Maharishi himself.

The digital option is in addition to the in person,

phone, and Zoom options. It makes use of the TM App, which was designed in 2021. The three one-hour app lessons are completed at the convenience of the student within a fifteen-day window of starting the TM practice. The app includes a meditation timer, which shows how much time has elapsed (vs. the iPhone timer, which shows how much time remains), and vibrates at the end. There are no startling gong or bells. The TM App has a calendar to log your meditations.

Having meditated most of my life, I have achieved a level of calm that is now just part of me. I know for certain that my TM practice helped me to exit more smoothly from an unhealthy relationship (see Lesson 4). TM is the best of the many tools in my toolbox.

TM's course fee includes lifetime follow-ups. The fee is income-based on a sliding scale. Students can receive two college credits, and healthcare professionals, such as nurses, licensed social workers, and massage therapists, can earn professional credits.

In my TM Teacher Training Course, we discussed why personal instruction is necessary when the TM technique itself is so simple. Why not just get a mantra off the internet and try to practice? Because simplicity needs to be taught, and without the teacher's guidance and the verification and validation of experiences, the student may become confused and may not gain the full benefit.

Most students have tried other techniques and never felt the level of calm they are longing for. But TM worked for them.

I am often asked by students how TM is different from other types of meditation. Generally, my response to this question is that TM is far easier to practice as well as far more effective at reducing stress and creating coherence in brainwaves.

No other meditation technique is able to reduce cortisol as much as the TM technique and has as many positive scientific research studies.

What I have learned from students who have tried other techniques is that those techniques require more focus and more effort when compared to the effortlessness of the TM technique. Students often report being frustrated by the effort of other techniques, and they find that their anxiety is increased instead of reduced.

One type of meditation called mindfulness involves a constant monitoring of the mind. Some meditators who have learned mindfulness report that they enjoyed it to a degree but longed for something more. Once they learned TM, they noticed a dramatic difference in the depth of their meditations. They noted that it took them a longer time to achieve a deeper state with mindfulness than with TM. Also, most people reported greater benefits outside of meditation with TM.

In fact, another teacher told me a story about a woman, who had been meditating with other techniques for over twenty years. She had been to India many times, went on long spiritual retreats, and learned probably every technique on the planet on a quest for inner peace, but to no avail. She was never truly satisfied.

During her first session of TM training, she was asked how she liked the TM technique. She replied in a stern voice, "It's an absolute tragedy." The teacher was taken aback by the answer since there was a long pause of silence and the teacher thought she might be in for a list of complaints. Instead, the new student continued, "It's as if I've never meditated before. Now this is meditation. This was truly profound."

She carried on speaking for a long time unable to understand why nothing she had ever done before took her to the depths of the mind like TM. She continues to be in awe of TM's simplicity and effectiveness. Her search was over. She finally found inner peace and began to enjoy life more.

Our main source of advertisement is a friend or family member raving about TM's benefits. People just need to try it for themselves. TM is an investment in your health. Once you have it, no one can ever take it away from you.

If we meditate regularly, we can become grounded in our higher self, find our purpose in life, and will notice that those tendencies toward control and not accepting things as they are will fall away. Many who have lived through extremely stressful events carry these negative thoughts into adulthood and they can create an unhappy life. Living your purpose offers deep fulfillment, and we become happy with who we are and what we have to offer to the world. TM can help everyone achieve just that.

#

Focus. Now more than ever, it's something most people struggle with. All the noise, distractions, and busyness of life cause stress, which can lead to burnout, forgetfulness, and further erode our ability to focus. Most people seek out TM to become more focused. Stress reduction leads to better focus. TM reduces stress.

Focus is a privilege, and most people need to have the intention to create a routine in order to cultivate it. In my TTC course, we were committed to our studies and our personal growth and helped each other reach the finish line. Our camaraderie and sense of community was priceless. It was a mature group and I was the youngest one.

Some women had a hard time being away from their family. I was fine as I had already been away from Laurina during her own TTC in Switzerland, and had been away at college for three years. I am probably too independent at times, but this is what makes me who I am. I felt honored to be walking in my parents' footsteps and become a second-generation TM teacher. If my future children let me teach them to meditate and become TM teachers, then that will be my true legacy.

I celebrated my twenty-third birthday shortly after we started in October 2009. My teachers and classmates decorated my bedroom door. The kitchen staff made a special meal. In the dining hall, everyone sang "Happy Birthday", and we ate cake.

The course wasn't always easy. Some days, the memorization and long videos felt endless. Other days, you felt on top of the world. We were meditating three times a day (the third time was ten minutes before lunch), and we were listening to forty years' worth of Maharishi videotapes. Maharishi always said students could meditate a little more.

Many of the lectures Maharishi has given have been recorded, so we learned the Vedic knowledge directly from him. All of the videotapes have since been transferred to DVDs or other digital products by MIU.

Sometimes, I would close my eyes during the videos and just listen, and could still take in the information. Learning the content was a challenge at times, but it taught me that when given the opportunity to be super focused, anything is possible. It felt peaceful.

The five months went by pretty quickly, and suddenly it was February 28, 2010. I became a TM teacher on Al's birthday. After graduation, students had a few days to finalize our plans and move out. It was a bittersweet goodbye. I was now ready to go out into the world and teach people the greatest gift that I had been given. However, I was also in the middle of completing my second semester of my MBA.

<<Laurina: Illus. Graduation for Olivia.>>

Even though I was able to apply the teacher training and some teaching projects to some elective credits and receive some real-life internship credit, my MBA program took two years instead of one. At some point, one of my professors and advisor asked me, "Olivia, when are you going to take some classes to complete your MBA?"

Well, I did complete everything by 2011 and graduated with a Green MBA, which specializes in lean management and sustainability. Lean management seeks to achieve small, incremental changes in processes to improve efficiency and quality over the long-term.

Instead of founding a company or working for a start-up, I began teaching TM full time in an inner-city high school in San Francisco. Although a career in fashion was still in the back of my mind, teaching TM at that point in my life felt like the right thing to do—especially after spending all that time taking the course.

The application process to place a teacher is rigorous, and fit is a strong consideration. At the time, it seemed that I was one of the only younger, ethnic TM teachers relatable enough to teach the diverse inner-city schoolkids. I applied for several positions, and received a few offers, including at a school in South Africa and from the inner-city high school in San Francisco. I had never been to San Francisco, but from movies and TV, it seemed like a cool city. I accepted the job.

#

OLIVIA LOPEZ

With focus, anything is possible. With my lifelong learning difficulties, the TM Teacher Training Course was one of the first times I learned something so complex with ease.

#

Here are my tips to help you improve your focus and achieve flow.

Tips for Lesson 3: With Focus, Anything Is Possible

1. Know your intention

    Be clear about what you want to accomplish and believe you can. Maharishi has a saying (in paraphrase): "What you put your attention on grows stronger" or "What you see, you become." It's so important to have a positive mindset and not always expect the worst.

2. Shut off your devices, especially while working

    We are bombarded by a constant flow of information from our electronic devices, distracting us from our intended pursuits. When you need to focus on a task, turn off your devices (or the notification feature)—and place them out of view. Just like seeing cookies can make us more likely to eat one, seeing our phone may tempt us to use it. Once distracted, according to a study by Professor Gloria Mark at the University of California, Irvine, "It takes an average twenty-three minutes and fifteen seconds to get back to the task." (Worker, Interrupted: The Cost of Task Switching, Kermit Pattison, Fast Company, July 28, 2008). And that's for *each* interruption.

3. Get adequate sleep

Lack of adequate sleep can lower alertness, slow thought processing, and reduce concentration. You may even become confused. Your ability to perform tasks related to reasoning and logic can be seriously affected. Chronically poor sleep hygiene further erodes your concentration and impacts memory.

My Transcendental Meditation students experience dramatic improvements in their sleep, even those with chronic sleep issues. They wake up less often during the night and have more REM sleep, and therefore wake up more refreshed. A study conducted at Sumitomo Heavy Industries by the Japanese National Institute of Industrial Health found that workers who learned the Transcendental Meditation Program fell asleep more easily at night, in comparison to control workers. (Japanese Journal of Industrial Health 32: 656, 1990).

4. Increase daily physical activity

Have you ever noticed how vigorous exercise leaves you feeling more relaxed and energetic throughout the day? When you don't move, your muscles can become tense. You may feel tightness in your neck, shoulders, and chest and it can affect your concentration. It's important to move your body daily, especially in the morning. Even a ten- to twenty-minute walk will help increase your energy and lower stress. Also, if you have a desk job, try getting up every thirty to sixty minutes.

5. Develop healthy eating habits

What we eat contributes to how we feel, including our mental sharpness and clarity. Omega-3 fatty acids and other essential fatty acids fuel your brain and protect against memory loss and lack of concentration. Low-fat and other restrictive diets, and even missed meals, can cause hunger, dehydration, cravings, and weakness that derail concentration. At the other extreme, rich foods, overeating, and excessive alcohol consumption can also challenge our memory and ability to focus. Notice how different foods affect your concentration. Eat balanced, nourishing meals. Follow your body's natural hunger cues.

6. Create your environment

Depending on what you are doing, the environment can affect your focus. A room that is too hot or too cold. Loud noises or complete silence. Strong odors or sweet aromas. Flashing lights or dimness. Your setting can impact your ability to focus. Build your environment thoughtfully, such as playing soft music or diffusing an essential oil (try lavender for relaxation or peppermint for stimulation), to promote concentration and help you stay on task.

7. Take responsibility for your mental health

Anxiety and depression, grief, and trauma drain our energy and make it difficult to focus. Diminished clarity is often temporary, with proper help. Seek out professional support and guidance to address any concerns that are weighing you down. If one counselor is not a good fit for you, try another one. Unburden your heart. Recovery is possible. Sometimes we need more than family and friends to find our own solution and give us the proper tools.

8. Watch the clock

The Ayurveda clock divides the day (and night) into three four-hour periods: 10:00–2:00, 2:00–6:00, and 6:00–10:00. Each period is best for specific activities. For example, the optimal time to meditate, problem-solve, and pursue creative projects is between two and six (both a.m. and p.m.). The best mealtime for the largest meal of the day is at noon or no later than 2 p.m. for maximum digestion, while the sun is at its highest point in the sky. Scheduling commitments during the most productive natural time promotes balance and ease, and enhances your focus on that task.

Increased focus paves the way for greater achievement. You can increase your ability to focus through a range of improved wellness regimens, like adequate sleep and a healthy diet, and directed goals, such as setting your intention and seeking professional help. Each requires you to take initiative.

LESSON 4
Be Flexible and Adaptable

Teaching TM Coast-to-Coast

If you feel like you're losing everything, remember
that trees lose their leaves every year and they
still stand and wait for better days to come.

Unknown

Balance, calm, and adaptability will help to manage all the twists and turns that life has to offer.

Although I had done some Transcendental Meditation teaching in Fairfield and Chicago, my first big, real-world TM job was with the Center for Wellness and Achievement in Education (CWAE), based in San Francisco. Fall 2010, I helped start a TM program at an inner-city public high school in the Mission District. TM had been introduced three years prior at the middle school level at Visitacion Valley Middle School in Visitacion Valley, in southeast San Francisco. I helped out there, too, when they needed me.

Teaching TM to students from diverse economic, social, and cultural backgrounds was extremely rewarding. Most of my students, aged ten to eighteen, had problems at home that were out of their control and created a lot of stress. During Quiet Time, as the TM program for schools is known, we practiced TM twice a day for fifteen minutes. Quiet Time gave my students reliable peace, quiet, and nourishment. School became a safe zone, a reprieve from their often chaotic homelife. The change in my students was profound, and the scientific research is compelling.

Practicing TM is good for everyone, but especially for students under high stress. It creates alpha brain wave coherence. Alpha brain waves are associated with restfulness, and coherence is associated with improved mental functioning. TM helps the student's brain to develop more quickly and to be more adaptable and resistant to stress.

Visitacion Valley has one of the highest crime rates in San Francisco. A UC Berkeley public policy professor summarized the effect of TM in the middle school for the *San Francisco Chronicle*: "In the first year of the Quiet Time Program, the number of suspensions fell by 45 percent. Within four years, the suspension rate was among the lowest in the city. Daily attendance rates climbed to 98 percent, well above the city wide average. Grade point averages improved remarkably." ("Meditation transforms roughest San Francisco schools", San Francisco Chronicle, January 12, 2014).

In 2014, when the program had been underway for seven years, Visitacion Valley Middle School students scored higher for happiness than any other school in San Francisco, regardless of socioeconomic background, on the annual California Health kids survey ("It's about time for Quiet Time", Scott Cawelti, Waterloo-Cedar Falls Courier, January 11, 2015). This article goes on to explain that the prime source of happiness at Visitacion Valley was the Quiet Time, a stress reduction program implemented at several Bay Area middle and high schools.

One of the most compelling stories from Visitacion Valley Middle School, was of a girl whose uncle was found shot one morning. Instead of staying with the family, she ran to school covered in blood. The teacher thought the blood was paint and scolded her for coming to school like that, only to discover the only way she could deal with the trauma of her uncle's death was to do Quiet Time with the group. She ran to try and make it in time, but arrived a few minutes late.

Another student was hearing gunshots on her way to school and Quiet Time was the only way to cope with her daily trauma of not knowing what to expect when she walks out the door.

#

I was beginning to understand my true gifts and calling in life: an empathic and understanding teacher who truly cares about her students and a solution-oriented friend who's always there for them.

After three years of teaching stints in the San Francisco schools for CWAE, I was ready for a change. Being with my students was rewarding, but could also be taxing—even with summers off. Teaching in inner-city public schools definitely doesn't get enough credit. I became close to many of my students and understood their significant life challenges. Even teaching TM in non-school settings can be taxing. You can only give from what you have and need to take care of yourself.

Having completed the 2012–13 school year, I was in Chicago visiting Laurina and Bolton. One day, Bolton's friend stopped by and mentioned to me the next annual TTC was beginning in the fall. They were looking for someone to assist with the course. I was intrigued, especially since I had enjoyed my own training so much. The next day, I got an email from one of my training teachers asking if I'd like to be the TTC assistant teacher in Vedic City.

I was thrilled, and again felt an intuitive pull to apply. I wanted to relisten to the forty years of Maharishi videos and support others through their training. My job was to make sure the course participants had everything they needed for the five-month program.

I remembered what I had enjoyed most about TTC: having a routine. I woke up between five and six and was in bed by ten. My meals were provided. Most evenings I had off.

I did a lot of food shopping off campus for items not offered by the cafeteria. As the TTC assistant teacher, I was in charge of leading the morning classes and keeping the classroom and common areas tidy. I also found it rewarding to help the class study for and pass the tests. One of my best friends was taking the course, so sometimes it was hard to always be in the teacher role and not the friend role. I led the youngest group and also the chattiest. They didn't always want to study (it's a lot of memorization and repetition), but with chocolate, coffee, chai tea, and a few jokes, we powered through.

#

In 2014, shortly before the group graduated, I was at another crossroads. A colleague and high school friend asked me if I had any interest in moving to San Diego to help open and teach at a second TM Center in Mission Valley, which is close to downtown San Diego. (The primary San Diego TM Center was thirty minutes north, in the wealthy beach town of Encinitas.)

I had always loved San Diego, and since my half-siblings were there, I thought why not? My half sister Sarah said San Diego has the most perfect weather all year around. I packed up in Fairfield and moved back to California.

I lived in the Encinitas TM Center, a beautiful two-story building designed according to the principles of Vedic architecture.

Vedic architecture, also known as Sthapatya Veda, is an ancient body of knowledge about how to build a house in harmony with the environment, so that the owners gain the maximum benefit from natural law, and therefore experience ideal health, prosperity, and happiness. The rules of Sthapatya cover things such as orientation of the house, the location of various activities in the house, materials used to build the house, and various formulas and ratios for the dimensions of the different rooms in the house.

Downstairs were a few teaching rooms, a large lecture

hall that also served as a meditation room, and a kitchen and dining room. Upstairs were four wings, which served as the teachers' private living quarters.

The other resident colleagues, a family of three, were like kin. I had gone to high school with the son, who was a few years younger than me. My dad knew the dad from his San Diego days. Although this family spent the most time preparing to launch the Mission Valley TM Center in San Diego, I did help with the last-minute touches and the grand opening. We also had an open house and invited all existing TM meditators in the area. I was brought in primarily to help teach once the Mission Valley location was up and running.

Another advantage of living at the Encinitas TM Center was that unless I was teaching at the Mission Valley TM Center, I didn't have to commute. Most of the administrative work for TM is done from home, so unless we were giving a TM Intro class, teaching TM, or providing TM follow-up, I didn't need to be on-site. Depending on the traffic on I-5, my commute either took twenty-five minutes or up to an hour.

The biggest plus, though, was the proximity to the ocean. The Encinitas TM Center was five minutes from the beach. I ran on the beach most mornings.

A few months after the new center opened, there was still

not quite enough teaching for the four of us, so I was asked if I could fill in as a teacher in Los Angeles that summer. I left in June for LA. I really liked it and had so many more friends there than in San Diego. The TM community in LA is large and active. Three local TM centers host frequent group meditations and other events. Many friends from Fairfield had also ended up in LA for various reasons. After a trial month, I was asked if I would consider joining the Beverly Hills TM Center full time.

#

Fall 2014, I moved to Los Angeles. Luckily, I was able to make just a few driving trips between San Diego and LA in my silver 2007 Toyota Camry. Not shipping my car and a lot of boxes was much easier. I sublet a friend's beautiful apartment in Beverly Hills and took care of her cat Henry. Can you tell I move a lot and am kind of a modern gypsy? I'll make your head spin telling you how many places I've lived. My grandma Trudy jokes that there's no more room in her address book for me.

Everything in Beverly Hills was pretty and shiny. The TM Center was a small, 1940s, three-bedroom two-bath, quaint house on South Wetherly Drive, not far from the corner of Beverly Wilshire Boulevard and Rodeo Drive, and just down the street from a Maserati dealership.

The bedrooms were used as meditation instruction rooms, and the living room was used for TM Intro talks and group meditations, and as office space for our three part-time administrative office assistants. With no central air-conditioning, on hot and humid days, we had to talk over the window AC units and fans. Being naturally soft-spoken, I had to use my louder teaching voice.

Our local TM community loved coming to group events and meditations. Every Thursday at 7:00 p.m. and Saturday at 11:00 a.m., TM practitioners from all over LA would come to Beverly Hills to meditate in a group. When you meditate in a group, especially in a large one, as I discovered in middle school, you can feel yourself go deeper and have a better experience. Once in a group of about forty, I went so deep in my meditation that I drifted off and thought I was at home in bed. Suddenly, our twenty minutes were up. I opened my eyes and was surprised to see the crowd of people in the room.

During my stint in Beverly Hills, I did see and meet some celebrities. I once saw Paris Hilton randomly. In the beginning, I was sometimes starstruck, but realized they are just normal people like the rest of us. I taught actors, writers, producers, singers, teachers, nurses, doctors, and children over the age of five—people from all walks of life and backgrounds. I had the honor of teaching some of the most hardworking, down-to-earth people in Hollywood.

I was at the TM center every day from 9:00 or 10:00 a.m. until 8:00 or 9:00 p.m., for group meditation or our evening follow-up meetings. Sometimes, I taught ten people in a day. Both individual instruction and group follow-up last an hour or two. Some students, like stay-at-home moms and retirees, would attend a group at 10:00 or 11:00 a.m., but most came at night after work. The meetings could start as late as 7:30 or 8:00 p.m.

I took meal breaks and was able to leave to run errands or get a blowout or mani-pedi. I wanted to look the part of a stylish California girl and a polished professional, even when my personal time was limited. When you look good, you feel good. I believe students appreciate when their teacher has taken the time to look put together. Laurina used to say that people respect you more when you don't look like you just rolled out of bed.

In TTC, I was taught to always, wherever I go, carry myself as a representative of TM. In the '70s when most of the TM teachers wore $300 suits, but also drove $300 cars, Maharishi said on video, "Your suit can be cheap, but it must be well cut!"

One day, a lady walked into our TM center with her service

dog for her appointment to learn TM. Getting to the Beverly Hills TM Center isn't always easy. The traffic and finding a parking space can be stressful. The lady announced that she was having a panic attack, but was excited to learn TM to cope with her anxiety. I gave her some time to rest and relax in our waiting room. Just being in the calm of the TM center and waiting, she started to feel better.

I brought her and her service dog into my office. After talking and getting to know her better, I prepared her for learning TM and then took her and her dog into one of the teaching rooms. After the first meditation, she felt so calm and couldn't believe how relaxed she could feel.

The next day, when she came back for her first of three follow-up meetings, again she couldn't believe what happened. She said that after her meditation, she no longer craved and needed the marijuana she usually smoked for pain and anxiety. She also slept much deeper that night. And her meditation showed up as light sleep on her Fitbit tracker.

The next morning, she made her smoothie and so had taken some steps, and then sat down to meditate for twenty minutes. Again, her Fitbit said she was sleeping lightly during her meditation. She came in so excited to share this with the group, passing her phone around. When we sleep, we have a combination of light, deep, and REM sleep. Her heart rate and pulse during meditation were tracked as if in light sleep, even though she was awake. This shows how much deep rest one can experience with TM. As the week progressed, she continued to feel better and better.

A few years later, she wrote to me, "It's been 1,250 days since I stumbled through the door of the TM center in the middle of a panic attack—and you were so amazing to me. I haven't missed a day since! Thank you for helping change my life."

Hearing her and other students' positive experiences is the most rewarding part of my job and why I continue to teach TM. To support students and help maintain their TM practice, all TM centers offer follow-ups. Students who attend follow-ups once a month for the first year, progress better than those who don't.

> While I was in California, both in San Francisco and L.A., I was fortunate to do a lot of work with the David Lynch Foundation. This organization was founded in 2005 by David Lynch, the world-famous film director, who has been practicing TM himself since 1973. Lynch describes his

experience with TM on the foundation's web site:

I started Transcendental Meditation® in 1973 and have not missed a single meditation ever since. Twice a day, every day. It has given me effortless access to unlimited reserves of energy, creativity and happiness deep within. This level of life is sometimes called "pure consciousness"—it is a treasury. And this level of life is deep within us all.

But I had no idea how powerful and profound this technique could be until I saw firsthand how it was being practiced by young children in inner-city schools, veterans who suffer the living hell of post-traumatic stress and women and girls who are survivors of terrible violence.

TM is, in a word, life changing for the good.

If you don't already meditate, take my advice: Start. It will be the best decision you ever make. (David Lynch, https://www.davidlynchfoundation. org/message.html)

The goal of the David Lynch Foundation is to make this technique available to individuals exposed to high stress.

While in L.A., I experienced first hand the great support David Lynch has gained from some of the great artists and entertainers in Hollywood. I attended several of the fundraising events, which included appearances by Jerry Seinfeld, Ellen DeGeneres, Paul McCartney, Katy Perry, and Russell Brand. I got to see first hand the positive effect TM has on inner-city school students. It's amazing to think that this organization has been responsible for bringing TM to more than 500,000 individuals throughout the world since its founding.

Here are some of the experiences of various celebrities with Transcendental Meditation.

> "Meditation has been a great tool for me in my life. It helps to quiet my mind and helps me see things more clearly. It brings a sense of peace to my day…. Meditation provides me space to re-balance and re-focus when things are at their busiest…. I feel a big difference in my mood when I practice regularly. I love it! It helps us become more aware; it brings wisdom and healing…. I have been meditating since

my early 20s and I must say that words do not express enough the significance of its gifts in my life." — Giselle Bundchen, producer and fashion model.

"How Transcendental Meditation Keeps Gisele Bündchen at the Top of Her Game",

People Magazine, May 5, 2017

"Through meditation on a daily basis, I get to strip away the masks that we build—that I build for myself, small and large—to reach the feeling of my true self. 'Oh, this is who I really am! This is how I can experience life!' My guiding principle has become being true to myself. I used to have lots of rules… No more." — Hugh Jackman, actor.

https://tmhome.com/hugh-jackman-meditation-changed-my-life/

"I start the day with Transcendental Meditation. It puts me in the best mood. I wake up and just prop myself up in bed for 20 minutes. It's the only time my mind gets absolute rest….It's changed my life, it's changed how I think about things. I meditate before I write a song before I perform. I feel my brain open up and I feel my most sharp. When I do it, I literally can feel the neuropathways in my mind opening up. It's almost like a halo is created around my head and things just start vibrating again." — Katy Perry, singer

https://tmhome.com/katy-perry-singer/

"I learned TM, the Transcendental Meditation technique. And it was exactly what I needed! The thing that blew me away the most about it was that it was the easiest thing I've ever done—not the easiest meditation, but the easiest thing I have ever learned. And I learn a lot of things, you know; that's my job! TM is so simple to learn; it's so simple to practice. Yet the amount of restoration that comes to you—the benefit across your life—well, it has changed everything." — Cameron Diaz, actress

https://tmhome.com/tm-meditation-for-cameron-diaz/

"I've been doing Transcendental Meditation for over 40 years…. Doing TM will help you to take things more easy…. Do you know how I was describing TM to somebody? It's like having… you know, your phone has a charger, right? It's like having a charger for your whole body and mind. That's what Transcendental Meditation is!" — Jerry Seinfeld, comedian and actor

https://tmhome.com/jerry-seinfeld-video-on-transcendental-meditation-a-charger-for-your-body-and-mind/

#

I thought the grass would be greener in LA, and it was for a while. But after three years there and teaching almost three hundred new students a year, I was burned out again. It was hard for me to keep up with the number of students in LA wanting to learn TM, with only so many hours in the day to accommodate them and their schedules. I always felt I had to service my students with individual follow-up meetings and be there for all the group meditations.

Although I love the social aspects and providing something so peaceful to my students, not taking enough time to rest took a toll on my health. Although when healthy, I do have good energy and endurance, I started feeling tired and was gaining stress weight from not exercising and eating meals at random times of the day.

March 2017, my male colleague and I had a miscommunication that led to some irreconcilable differences in how we managed the center and in our teaching styles. I felt my time there was coming to an end. Meanwhile, a recent graduate of the TTC in Bali (whom I'll refer to as D) joined our center in LA. It's customary for experienced TM teachers (I was seven years in) to mentor new teachers and show them how a TM center is run. D and I had already been talking for a few months before he arrived. We were excited to work with each other.

Instead of leaving LA for a slower pace elsewhere, more lifestyle balance, and a more compatible teaching partner, I was mentoring D. He was cute and said that he had been crushing on me ever since he watched a video of me years back. There are lots of couples in the TM world, including Laurina and Bolton. Dating a fellow TM teacher is not frowned upon in our organization; it is not uncommon.

The relationships don't always work out, such as Laurina and Al's. It's like running a small business together and navigating a personal life, too. Even when you divide the tasks to run a TM center, it's hard to agree on everything. I was good at managing the administrative side, but D had an opinion about everything. He tried to change things to better appeal to a younger audience, which was good, but I was used to our established guidelines. We butted heads a lot.

March 2017, TM teaching slowed down in LA, and D became bored. He suggested that he and I move to Florida to start fresh and open a new TM center from scratch. I was intrigued to explore this possibility. In 2014, someone had told D about TM. He found the research on the health benefits compelling, and a few months later, learned TM in Sarasota, Florida. (Currently, you need to be meditating for at least two years before enrolling in teacher training.)

D had stayed in touch with his teacher, who told him they needed more young teachers in Florida. June 2017, during the rainy season, we visited Orlando. Coming from California where it barely rains and not loving how the rain ruins my hair and makeup, I wasn't convinced Florida was the place for me. But everyone said that people move there for the winters and most of the year is sunny and beautiful, and they were right.

#

August 2017, I moved across the country with a guy I had just met. Some of my friends were concerned, but I was ready for a fresh start again. Overall it turned out pretty well—for the most part. We opened a TM center in Orlando, and then in 2019, we were asked to also cover coastal cities about two to three hours from Orlando: Saint Petersburg, where we lived, and Clearwater; and during the coronavirus pandemic, even taught in Sarasota (about an hour south of Saint Petersburg).

Over three years, D and I taught over a thousand people and helped existing practitioners reconnect with their TM practice. There hadn't been a full-time teacher in Orlando for a long time, so people were very happy we were there. We were going strong, and I was healthier than I had been in LA, but now had an opposite problem to overwork and burnout.

When it was slow, it was really slow, and there was not enough money to live on. TM teachers are paid a commission on the number of new students they teach. We are not salaried. Our compensation level is similar to that of a schoolteacher and can range from $20,000 to $50,000 a year depending on many factors. Nothing is guaranteed. We pay for housing, unless we are living in a house that we are also able to use as a TM center.

The TM organization helped D and me get started financially when we moved to Florida; then we switched to a different business model. We paid our own expenses and received a higher commission. This made it a little easier to make more money after our expenses. Whatever D and I brought in together, we split evenly. I wanted things to be fair, unlike in other centers that don't pool income. It was still a struggle sometimes not knowing how many people we would teach and if we were going to be able to pay our business expenses and then our personal expenses.

Running a TM center is like owning a small business. We are independent contractors, known as "1099" after the IRS tax form 1099-MISC. We can write off our business expenses, but lack the stability and security of a salaried job. For D and I, the financial stress led to relationship stress. Then the coronavirus pandemic happened.

#

Moving across the country, starting a new business, and moving in with a partner was a lot of change at once. I learned to be flexible and adaptable, but the stress could be overwhelming at times. Here are my tips that helped me cope and may help you, too.

Tips for Lesson 4: Be Flexible and Adaptable

1. Lose the fear and worry

    Release the grip of dread and panic. Take five deep, even breaths. Find the least amount of stress that fuels your energy. Most of my opportunities in life came easily and naturally. After my TM Teacher Training Course, I had three job offers and every TM teaching opportunity led to the next. When I was in a flow state and staying in the present moment, things came to me more easily.

2. Accept change

    Everything changes, so expect change in your life and embrace it. During the coronavirus pandemic, many of us had to reinvent ourselves after business closures and job losses. Others saw the pandemic as an opportunity to try a different path, and joined the Great Resignation. I confronted several professional and personal obstacles. I had to manage my constant stress, and find a way around the roadblocks. Learning to surrender and go with the changes—rather than resisting—was one of my biggest lessons.

3. Drop the attachment to your things

My friends will attest to the fact that I am an organized hoarder. I believe that—one day—I will need each of these things that I have schlepped coast-to-coast for my entire adult life. This year, I warmed to the idea of minimalism and detachment. I moved back home with Laurina and Bolton, gave up my car lease, and took an extended summer break. I was still recovering from having ended the relationship with D. I had to surrender and trust that letting go was what I needed to transform. Living with less and making fewer decisions has been freeing and has opened up space for better opportunities. Let go of the old and welcome the new really rings true here.

4. Rewire the brain through the TM technique

By reducing stress, TM allows all parts of the brain to work in concert, called "brain wave coherence." For example, our prefrontal cortex is like the CEO of our brain, responsible for problem-solving, concentration, and impulse control. The limbic lobe controls emotions, and so on. With better coordination, you will be more flexible and adaptable, and your problem solving and decision-making abilities will improve

5. Be willing to learn

We never really stop learning, so be open to learning new methods and ways of doing things in all aspects of your life. Be open to new ideas, new ways of thinking, new tools, and new technologies. Try to approach something you've always done a certain way differently.

6. Improvise

Don't overthink and second-guess everything that you do. Practice being spontaneous—change your weekend plans, accept that last-minute invitation. Grab the opportunity; it might not come again.

Have an optimistic mindset and maintain a de-stressing practice, such as TM. When you are balanced and calm and less rigid and grasping, you will be better able to maneuver life's twists and turns with ease and grace.

LESSON 5
Understand Your Needs and Ask for Support and Guidance

Coming Home

If the version of you from 5 years ago could see you right now, they'd be proud. Keep going.

Unknown

Seek help and guidance to learn who you are and understand what you need. Explore what it means to be you.

When the coronavirus pandemic began, D and I were still living in Saint Petersburg and working full time at the TM center in Orlando. Even though I had a colleague, I took on a lot of the administrative work. I was good at it and particular about how it should be done. I was also teaching TM, providing the gift of inner peace to others, and yet, I wasn't creating enough time for sunshine, exercise, and fun for myself.

Even when you love your job, it can be draining. The high social interaction of my job took its toll. I suffered burnout, which led to other health issues that I am still trying to balance. I learned the hard way to take my health more seriously. Without good health and energy, I didn't have much to give others.

When I took a Myers-Briggs test in college, I finally discovered that I'm an introvert. In college, I had envied the extroverted girls who could socialize all the time and never seemed to need alone time. I wanted to be out and about connecting with others, but also needed alone time. I could spend days by myself, in silence doing my own thing. I have learned that smaller, more intimate group settings and being with friends are better for me than being in large groups of acquaintances or among strangers in a crowd.

In some romantic relationships, I have felt like the over giver and even a people pleaser, I am still learning to have a more even balance of give-and-take. I believe when you meet the right person, most of the time, the relationship will be effortless. I've had to learn to set more boundaries, even with my best friends and other loved ones, and spend more time by myself.

As an only child, I learned early on to entertain myself. I am still very independent, almost to a fault. I am learning to receive more and to accept more help from people. More than ever, during the coronavirus pandemic, I have learned to accept my mother Laurina's unflagging love and support. In the past, my boyfriends were sometimes intimidated by our closeness. If someone loves you unconditionally, even if you find it annoying at times, receive it and appreciate it.

I have friends of all ages and backgrounds, but Laurina is truly my best friend. She raised me on her own for over fifteen years. We had only each other for half my life, and we are only twenty-four years apart.

Love from a parent isn't always a given. Finding one's life purpose also isn't a given. I feel blessed to have both.

#

TM Then and Now.

Sixty-plus years have passed since the founding of the TM organization, and yet, a lot about TM remains the same. Students still learn one-on-one with a teacher. Same-gender teaching is still preferred, but no longer required. Most classes are still taught in person, although online options are now also available. The technique is still practiced twice a day, about fifteen to twenty minutes each session. There is considerable outreach to a wide range of prospective students of all ages and in particular, at-risk populations.

As science continues to prove the benefits of meditation, Western cultures increasingly embrace awareness techniques; and as technology has advanced, much has moved online, and interest in TM has flourished. When I became a TM teacher in 2010, TM online meditation groups were not even a thing yet. TM teachers can now connect virtually with students anywhere in the world.

In March 2020, when the world shut down due to the coronavirus pandemic, the TM organization needed to adapt. I had to take three months off from teaching until I was deemed an essential worker in the state of Florida. I was able to do meditation check-ins via Zoom, but not teach. Online platforms are more convenient for the student and accessible to more people. The development and launch of the app and Zoom sessions were expedited due to the pandemic. Now there is a hybrid teaching process of partially in person and digital self-study course.

Virtual group meditations boomed in all areas including apps and Zoom options. Also in March 2020, Bob Roth, CEO of the David Lynch Foundation, started leading a twice-daily group meditation on Zoom. According to its website, the foundation's mission is to help "prevent and eradicate the all-pervasive epidemic of trauma and toxic stress among at-risk populations through . . . TM." (David Lynch Foundation, Center for Resilience, "About Us," https://www.davidlynchfoundation.org/about-us.html. Accessed 28 November 2021). Other than Roth's and individual teachers' sites, there is not yet a dedicated TM channel for live meditations.

Due to the Maharishi Effect (see Lesson 2), group meditations in person or remotely have been shown to increase harmony and peace in the environment.

December 2021, state by state, small TM in-person meetings resumed. But the way we teach TM and the ability to meditate on the phone or Zoom has forever changed. I started helping lead Laurina's online yoga and daily group meditations. I've also been able to reconnect more easily with my students around the country.

Some meditators working by Zoom and other online meeting platforms all day have Zoom fatigue and don't want to meditate by phone or computer. Most, though, have found the benefit of having a remote option. They feel a sense of community, connection, and accountability to be part of an online meditation group.

Here's to the future of meditation, keeping the technique pure and traditional, and also making it easy and practical for students to learn the TM technique and strengthen their practice.

#

If I Could Do Anything. . . March 2020, when the coronavirus pandemic shutdown began in America, my life changed— much for the good. My family started bi-weekly, two-hour Zoom meetings, and I felt less isolated in Florida.

D and I wanted to simplify our lives and lower our overhead, so we moved out of the house in Saint Petersburg into our new TM Center in Orlando. A few months later, June 2020, following problems with the landlord, we moved to Clearwater. Our new house was larger and cheaper, closer to the water and closer to my friends and clients. Since I hadn't returned to working full time yet (due to the pandemic), the move was smoother and settling in was quicker.

Soon after we settled in, D was invited on a special meditation course (like a retreat) for young men in West Virginia. I spent the summer mostly alone at our new Clearwater rental. I had a lot of time to think and to focus on myself, a rare and nice treat.

One day, I was talking on the phone with a friend I'd met in Florida. She told me some of her problems, and I gave her some insights and perspective. She said, "Wow, Olivia. You are so good at this. Maybe you should be a Life Coach!" I realized she was right. I was familiar with life coaching, having started on a personal journey with a Life Coach that summer. I took two courses with my Life Coach, to help answer one question: If I could do anything, what would I do?

As a TM teacher, I listen to people's anxieties and problems, and I'm able to offer the tool of meditation. TM helps them more easily reduce their stress so they can make better decisions. However, it's also important in life to have someone to hold you accountable and teach you new, healthy habits and routines. That's what a Life Coach can do. I was doing that with TM anyway, as my students would ask me about my lifestyle and self-care. My friends have always asked me for advice.

Spring 2021, I decided to become a holistic Life Coach. I already maintain an online health and wellness business and expanded my services to include health coaching. I have successfully led many people through our thirty days to healthy living program, which incorporates healthy lifestyle changes and clean nontoxic supplements.

OLIVIA LOPEZ

My goal is to help those seeking to become healthier and more fulfilled through improvements in their lifestyle. My mission in life is to help people help themselves through basic yet effective tools. This is also what inspired me to write this book for you.

When I was younger, before I became a TM teacher, I envisioned myself talking to the public and being on stage. I have spoken to large groups before and introduced guest speakers to large audiences. Once, I skipped saying part of someone's biography because I was intent on making eye contact with the audience and lost my place. Oops. Apparently, no one noticed but me (and maybe the physicist I was introducing).

I've always been told I have a strong presence and my friends have always complimented me on my calm, pleasant, and optimistic energy. I am definitely not high-strung and rarely get angry. When I do get annoyed or when I am stressed and get overwhelmed, I typically just want to be alone and have a hard time accepting help. Other times, I have felt alone with my problems and have a really hard time admitting I need help or guidance. These experiences have helped me relate better to others in need.

My biggest aspiration in life is to help people and help make them feel loved and appreciated. Many of us have not had support from parents or other significant people in our lives. Even though I have had my struggles in life and things I've worked through to overcome, I like to say they are first world problems. I am so grateful for the life I've had and all of my adventures and experiences.

My challenges have all shaped me so I can be that empathetic, understanding friend and teacher, who will also call you out and provide solutions for how you can change yourself to adapt to the situation and set boundaries. I have access to many tools that are not well known and underutilized. Some of them are ancient, such as Ayurvedic principles like lemon water in the morning and rising with the sun, and others are more modern, like red light therapy, which helps heal your cells and regulate your circadian rhythms. Each has helped me and my clients.

We can gain the knowledge to become our own health and wellness advocate. Now more than ever, it's important to protect ourselves from the increased pollutants in our water, food, and environment, as well as find fulfillment in life and surround ourselves with people who love, uplift, and support us. Sometimes that means making big changes. Like I did.

#

OLIVIA LOPEZ

Summer 2021, after eleven years, I left the only profession I had ever known. I ended a professional and romantic relationship (with D) that wasn't healthy for me at the time. I started focusing more intentionally on my health and routine, reconnected with friends and family, started accepting help to restore my health, and finally had time and inspiration to write this book. It was a lot of change for one summer.

As 2021 was coming to an end, at thirty-four years old, I felt the need to use this time to transform myself and come back home to myself. My truth. I love the quote from the Bhagavad Gita, "Curving back within myself, I create again and again." (Bhagavad Gita, Chapter 9, Verse 8). Only when we slow down and quiet our mind can we connect with our true and higher self. I had gotten caught up in the rat race professionally and needed to learn to slow down and take care of myself. I am grateful to Laurina and others, who guided me. I also had a lot of quality time with Al (my father) that summer, and felt like his little girl who he was trying to help and guide in the right direction.

And then, when I least expected it, I met an amazing man, the old-fashioned way—through an acquaintance, who now is like family and a great mentor. Tommy is exceeding my expectations of what a partner (and a healthy relationship) should be. Being in the right relationship with the right person can be so fulfilling. But you need to prepare yourself for it and be in the right space to receive it. Now after two years together, I can say I have healed so much and have been fully able to feel loved, accepted for who I truly am and safe in a relationship.

My two-plus decades of practicing Transcendental Meditation have been my best tool for self-development and have paved the way to all other self-development I have done over the years. If you are looking for Mr. or Ms. Right, I know it sounds cliché, but you need to love yourself first and focus on making yourself healthy and happy. In my experience, only then can God, the universe, or whatever energy force you believe in help you find that person and put you two together.

Right now, take a moment and close your eyes. Think of a few things that you are thankful for, and a few desires or wishes you would like to call in to your life. Do something for yourself today that brings you joy.

#

Here are my tips to help you understand your needs and ask for support and guidance.

Tips for Lesson 5: Understand Your Needs, and Ask for Support and Guidance

1. Get tested

    To learn more about yourself, your tendencies, and your path, read Gary Chapman's *The Five Love Languages* (1992), explore the Enneagram of Personality, or take the Myers-Briggs Type Indicator Test. To those familiar with the latter, have you guessed my personality type yet? It's INFP, which stands for introverted, intuitive, feeling, and perceiving.

2. Know your rhythm

    According to Ayurveda, every person is born with a particular mind-body constitution, or dosha. Your dosha represents its proportions of the five natural elements (fire, earth, air, water, and ether). Learning about your dosha will help you understand your needs and balance your health. Like increases like, so if you are pitta dosha, or fire- and water-element dominant, spicy food and hot weather will aggravate your natural constitution. Seek out the opposite quality to restore balance. Similarly, monitoring your pulse can detect and even correct imbalances. TM practitioners can enroll in online courses in self-pulse assessment through Maharishi International University.

3. Keep a daily gratitude journal

Feeling grateful can help you frame your experiences in a positive light. Every night before you go to bed, write down three things, experiences, or people you are grateful for. Writing longhand, by stimulating a collection of cells in the base of your brain known as the reticular activating system (RAS), helps our brain process information.

4. Stay connected with friends

During the coronavirus pandemic, I had more time to reconnect with friends. It was comforting to share our struggles during the pandemic and in our relationships. After moving so much and at times feeling lonely, it has been very nourishing having a group of girlfriends in the Sarasota area where I now live.

5. Have your chart done by a Maharishi Vedic astrologer

Jyotish[1] is an excellent tool to help us understand

---

[1] Maharishi Jyotish is the system of astrology I have been following most of my life. It is a scientific, mathematical system for predicting future events in our life, based on the knowledge of the laws of nature guiding the relationship between the planets and individuals. This ancient system of

ourselves and how the current planetary positions influence our happiness, success, and health. Every year, I have a reading with a Maharishi Vedic astrologer to help me navigate the coming months based on the tendencies of my planetary constellation. A general reading focuses on health, work, and relationships, but

---

knowledge can predict all aspects of our lives, including our health, our relationships, our career, our happiness, and our spiritual development.

The reason it is possible to predict changes in our lives based on the influences from planets is that we are all connected with the universe on a very deep level. Everything in the universe is connected through an underlying field of consciousness, or in physics, the unified field. Since everything is connected, then to fully understand our own lives, we need to understand many other aspects of the universe outside of ourselves as well. Fortunately, there are experts who already have studied the connections between the planetary influences and our own lives, and who have been trained to be able to make these predictions for us.

When we learn about future events and tendencies that are highlighted by Maharishi Jyotish, we can take steps to try to avoid or lessen the negative effect of those events and tendencies. The other helpful tool from this system is that it can select auspicious times to take on new activities, such as starting a new business, moving into a new home, or setting a date for a marriage.

The best source for setting up a consultation in Maharishi Jyotish is: www. maharishijyotishprogram.eu

you can ask anything that is relevant for you. In prior readings, I was told that the next few years would be challenging on many levels. Sometimes, we need to sit tight and let things unfold in their proper, astrological time. As I approach my new astrological subperiod, I am feeling lighter and more energetic than I did last year.

6. Consult with a psychologist, counselor, or Life Coach

In Lesson 3's tip 7, I recommend mental health counseling as a tool to free yourself from suffering and strengthen your focus. It is not a sign of weakness to seek help from a professional. Mental health is just as important as your physical health; in fact, they are connected. Here, I suggest that counseling can also be used to help you achieve specific goals, in all areas of your life. An objective professional can help identify self-defeating patterns of behavior and other obstacles to achieving your goals and feeling fulfilled. Many successful people seek out coaches, and even Life Coaches have coaches. I was inspired to become a Life Coach after my very positive experiences of working with one.

7. Listen to your body

What is your body asking for? Heed its call— whether for more rest or less sugar, more fun or less sitting. Take the time to do whatever your soul is yearning for. Honor your body's inner wisdom.

My seven tips for understanding your needs, and asking for support and guidance have a common thread: exploration. Be curious. Be patient. Go to the resources that will meet your needs.

LESSON 6
Let the Universe Provide the Answer

Let It Be

There's no need to rush. What's meant for you always arrives right on time.

Mandy Hale

Trust in yourself, have faith, and accept that the universe will provide the answers.

I was getting used to asking for help, but sometimes found it difficult to accept. I would get annoyed at Laurina, even though she offers great advice and it often proves right. I was learning to take a step back and trust that my best guidance is from within. We just need to be patient and listen. The universe will provide the answer.

Although I wanted to stay in Florida with Tommy when we first met, Laurina encouraged me to come back to Chicago and enjoy her beautiful home surrounded by nature. Her property is like a forest with big, old oak trees. Lake Michigan, with its breathtaking views, is just a few miles away. I could eat her healthy meals each day, take long walks, and have much needed discussions on many of the lessons I'm sharing with you. April 2021, Laurina flew to Florida to help me pack up my life, we shipped over twenty boxes and then fit as much as we could in my Toyota Camry and road tripped back to Chicago for the summer.

For the first time in many years, I had no responsibilities. I could hit pause, and breathe. During meals and on walks, I talked to Laurina and Bolton about the many things I was going through. Speaking about my experiences helped me process them and realize the deep lessons I needed to learn.

Tommy and I had just started dating before I left for Chicago. It was hard to leave him, but I knew I had to sort through my physical belongings and clear out the old karma back home and make room for new beginnings. As I struggled to regain my balance, I would, at times, feel shot down and defeated. At my lowest point, I thought that God or the higher powers in the universe were somehow against me. It was not true. In fact, I believe the universe rallied around me to create a circumstance of reflection, so that I could see the blessings in front of me—one of them being my new partner.

Tommy is a naturally happy, balanced and hardworking human being, a rare trait these days. While many of the rest of us are still searching for tools to reduce their stress, Tommy's life is mostly smooth sailing. He has lived a simple, pure, and good life. He comes from a good family, works very hard and has good role models in his parents. There's a saying that if you want to know how a man will treat you, see how he treats his mother and his sisters. Tommy has the utmost respect for his mother and sisters, his dad, me, and every human he encounters. People remark on his kindness, warmth, and integrity. I'm among the greatest beneficiaries of Tommy's goodness. So, when you think no one has your back—pause, pray, and watch the light emerge.

When I met Tommy, I wasn't looking for a boyfriend. Sometimes, God brings you what you need, not what you think you want. I couldn't be more grateful to have found true love during probably one of the most difficult years of my life.

#

It's important to evaluate our lives from time to time to determine our level of fulfillment and happiness. Of course, it's unrealistic that we will be experiencing a level ten every day. There are always peaks and valleys. You've probably heard the expression "it's the journey, not the destination" that is the most meaningful.

My whole life, friends have sought my advice and strangers have opened up to me, and so I feel it would be a disservice not to provide help to those who are seeking it. During the pandemic, my student Chrissey, a nurse, said, "TM saves my life, my family's and my patients' lives every single day. It is extremely easy to learn."

#

Gratitude and seeing all the good, instead of focusing on the negatives of life and of ourselves, are the keys to moving forward with dignity and grace. We are never going to have a perfect road map at all times to where our life is going. We all need to be flexible and adaptable. We need to stay settled within ourselves to clearly see the signs that are coming from the universe. When there is uncertainty, life can be hard. Surrender to your trust and faith in God or your higher power. Know you are not alone in this world.

Here are my tips to allow you to settle and let the universe provide the answer.

Tips for Lesson 6: Let the Universe Provide the Answer

1. Surrender with confidence

   When you let go of something, such as a belief, deep desire, material object, or partnership, trust that if it was meant to be in your life, it will find its way back. When we try to control or hold onto something, things usually don't go as planned. I've learned this time and time again. The only way to get what you want is to be unattached and let go. Then when you least expect it, your desire will be fulfilled. Have faith that everything will work out just fine.

2. Trust and believe in yourself

   Trust in yourself and your capacity to handle life. Sometimes, just from living our busy day-to-day lives, we lose our connection to ourselves, to nature, and our belief in what is possible. You can create the life you want. Start by adopting the lifestyle and routines you want. Surround yourself with people you admire.

Create the environment you need to feel and do your best. Envision your dreams. What we see, we become.

3. When in doubt, trust your intuition

Our greatest asset is our intuition, our gut feeling. We can rely on our intuition to help us navigate difficult situations and guide our decision making. Just like memory, critical thinking, and intellect, your intuition is a mental muscle you can strengthen and use to become the best possible, most successful version of yourself. Intuition can be strengthened through meditation, being in nature, and doing something active such as running, dancing, cooking, or even taking a shower. Movement can calm the cognitive mind and open up your intuition.

4. Fulfill your desires through quiet contemplation

Have you ever had a desire that immediately came true? Someone brings you a coffee just when you crave it, or you find the perfect outfit for an event in your size. When we are deeply settled and established in the core of our being, our desires are more likely to be fulfilled. We can increase the likelihood through meditation, prayer, and inner reflection.

5. Maintain your faith

Faith in God or a higher power in the universe is essential for all healing. Throughout my life, during each challenge, I have told myself, "God has better plans for me." I believe that God's timing is perfect.

Letting the universe provide the answer begins with going inward. With faith, trust, hope, and effort, we can find ourselves and our way home. Everything is connected.

LESSON 7
The Next Chapter

Your time is limited, so don't waste it living someone else's life. Don't be trapped by dogma—which is living with the results of other people's thinking. Don't let the noise of others' opinions drown out your own inner voice. And most important, have the courage to follow your heart and intuition.

Steve Jobs

I am only a few steps ahead of you

As you can see from reading about my life, you must realize that life in general is never constant. Our lives are ever changing and evolving, sometimes for the better or for the worse. It's important to navigate our lives more in the direction of things that bring us the greatest fulfillment, happiness, and ease in our life. You have probably heard the expression: "Life is a marathon not a sprint". We sometimes need to be patient with ourselves. Success and our own inner evolution can take time. You may not be where you want to be yet; however, you can let that fuel your passion and motivation to make things happen. Don't lose sight of being present in your daily life and learn to enjoy the ride. If you're feeling sad and frustrated that circumstances aren't in your favor, then surrendering to the outcome might help. That doesn't mean you don't try different solutions or try taking another path. Sometimes you need to be able to tap into your creativity and focus on the tasks at hand that can help you reach your goal, while simultaneously being unattached to the outcome.

On this journey, as I speak about people in my life, whether it's a boss or a former boyfriend who did not treat me well or who was controlling in some way, I realized that they had their own trauma causing that type of response.

I am not saying that we should ever stay in an abusive relationship, because we understand this person had some trauma that caused them to be abusive. But understanding the source of the abuse may help us and may allow us to forgive that person's negative actions.

We know the likelihood of these people changing is nearly impossible, so it's necessary to move on. And we should always value ourselves more, so that we can find people who are more balanced, loving, and supportive of us.

What has also been important in my journey is never to feel bitter or angry because of the things that have happened to me in the past. We always have free will to change our circumstances. At the same time I was writing this book, I saw an interview with Oprah and Viola Davis about Viola Davis' recent memoir about her life.

Viola Davis grew up in extreme poverty. She was also sexually abused by people that came to her house, and no one protected or defended her. Every day a group of boys would wait outside of school to beat her up and call her names, but she figured out a way to get out of school ahead of them and run fast to get home unharmed.

She also remembered times when her father would physically attack her mother. Even though her father beat her mother, she forgave her father later in life when she understood better the trauma in her father's life that led him to this behavior. But she also stuck up for her mother. The point is that we don't allow this abuse to happen. However, when the abuser stops the abusive behavior, there can be a level of forgiveness.

With all this turmoil in Viola's life, she still had the courage and belief in herself to become an extremely successful actress, one of the leading actresses of her generation.

From a young age, Viola loved acting. However, when she was about to go to college, she decided she didn't want to study acting in college since she didn't think you could make very much money in an acting career, and she was determined not to live in poverty. But her sister convinced her that it made no sense not to study the one thing she loved the most. The lesson is that if you are passionate about something, the likelihood of you making money over time is there, but it won't happen if you never try.

What if she had not pursued acting? We wouldn't have this amazing actress today. It just shows what belief in yourself and courage will do.

The other lesson from Viola Davis is that we always have to put our lives in perspective, knowing that someone else could have it much worse than we did. I explained earlier in my book about how I was bullied but nowhere near the extent of Viola Davis.

No matter what our circumstances, it's very important that we believe in ourselves, that we take charge of our lives, that we pursue our dreams with courage, that we have faith, and then we will find our true happiness within.

#

I have always been drawn to ways I can help people evolve and grow in happiness in their lives. In recent years, I have developed an interest in the field of life coaching. This is a field that has grown to become a powerful way for people to attain their goals and fulfil their dreams in life more easily.

My friends have told me over the years that I am a great friend, listener, and give thoughtful advice and recommendations. About a year ago, one of them suggested that I should investigate becoming a Life Coach. One day, while we were on the phone, after she was telling me about some challenges in her life, I was giving her some different ways of viewing the situation and offering some advice on how she could manage it. She then said, "Wow, Olivia you are so good at this." It was in that moment I knew I had to take this seriously and help more people than just my friends and existing clients. I officially became a Life Coach in 2021, but I feel that I have been coaching and helping people most of my life.

When I worked with my Coach Dr. Onalee in 2020, I did

some deep inner work. First, we worked on self-love, then forgiveness—forgiving yourself and forgiving others. Then we worked on mindset, setting boundaries, healing our relationship with our parents as well as inner child work just to name a few techniques. When we heal the past, then we can bust through our limiting beliefs and move forward and attract better things to us. We also focus on our dream life and what actions we can take to attract and attain it. It's the small daily habits that create lasting change in our lives. If we add routines and have trackers and schedules, it's much easier to stick to new habits. And it's important to make them fun too.

During my coaching with Dr Onalee, I started seeing changes immediately. I was able to realize I was outgrowing some relationships and needed to love and take care of myself better. I started taking action steps towards my goals, even though some were very difficult: going through a breakup, taking a break from a 10-year profession that was my only profession after college and being so identified with it, finding who I am and what I want in life, moving home to Chicago temporarily, then moving back to Sarasota to build a new life with my boyfriend. Then I took on a job just to work and it wasn't aligned with my future goals, and I felt stressed again. I felt like I had to take it to earn money to support myself, but quickly realized this wasn't my passion. I needed to set boundaries for myself and finally let go. It wasn't a job I could just quit, I needed to train a replacement. After that last day of training, I was so relieved. This experience taught me to never put my needs aside. It's never worth sacrificing your health and well-being; especially when you feel you aren't being appreciated or valued. I knew this book wasn't going to write itself and it's very hard to be creative when you are stressed and tired. I learned my lesson!

As I write this last chapter of my book, I finally feel things are falling into place. I can say it's been a whirlwind these past two years. Lots of moving, traveling, healing, diving deep, and trying to take small action steps every day to stay healthy. I have met some amazing people and have found some jobs I can work while I build my coaching business that get me out of the house and around like-minded people, which brings me joy. My health is slowly getting better, and I feel my natural reserves of energy are finally emerging again. I am practicing more self-love, self-acceptance, and nourishing my body so I can be my best self, so I can serve humanity.

Over the years I have coached many friends and clients in different ways, by just offering a safe nonjudgmental space for someone to share what they are going through. I helped one friend transition out of a narcissistic toxic relationship and go on to attract her soul mate to her. Now they are engaged. Another I gave dating advice to while she was navigating the dating scene. Another lost 75 pounds, started sleeping through the night, and started her own business. Recently, I helped another friend clean up her finances and connected her with a financial adviser to help her get out of debt as well as launch her Airbnb Business. Helping people is so rewarding. It's truly an indescribable feeling and for me its so effortless.

So, what is life coaching?

Life Coaches help their clients in improving their relationships, careers, and day-to-day lives. They work with you to change, re-direct and navigate your life, uncover your desires, take steps towards your goals, achieve your dreams, bust limiting beliefs, and identify roadblocks. They can also offer deeper, more holistic approaches looking at the bigger picture of the mind, body, and soul connection.

Group Coaching

I found my coaches have helped inspire me to make the changes for myself, especially the group coaching programs. Group coaching is a program where you meet weekly in a group online to follow up on an assignment you may have received individually from your coach. When you check in with your group weekly, it can be easier for accountability to hit your weekly goal, knowing that you will be sharing your progress. You will also develop friendships with others in the group that can continue even after the program has finished. I am still friends to this day with people I met in group coaching programs.

In life coaching, a key component is to understand your "why", which is discovering your true motivations or aspirations, and being able to incorporate those deep motivations and aspirations in your life work. Understanding your "why" is important because it helps to inspire you to get from where you are to where you want to be. For me, I learned that my "why" was drawing me further into this field of life coaching, where I could learn and offer techniques for self-development to other people, while living my purpose.

When we understand our own "why", it makes it easier for us to take steps towards our goal. For example, if we learn that our "why" is to have more energy and happiness in our life, what are the tools we would need to get there? A Life Coach will often begin by helping you identify your own "why", since they know this is critical to helping you make progress towards your goals. Sometimes you may need help identifying your own "why", and Life Coaches are experienced in helping you uncover this knowledge.

Another aspect of life coaching is related to health. Many Life Coaches will also give you advice on how to improve your health, and they will give you an understanding of how you can improve your mind-body connection. This concept of "mind-body" is the idea that the mind can affect the body in a positive or negative way, just as the body can affect the mind in a positive or negative way. These two aspects of life are intimately connected, so it's important to understand how that connection can be improved.

For example, when I work with clients, I will incorporate Ayurveda and a 30 day Clean Eating Program, which focuses on gut health, and healthy nutrient dense meals.

How are Life Coaches different from psychotherapists?

Life Coaches are not psychologists or psychotherapists. They don't have specific training to deal with psychological disorders. Instead, they are very good problem solvers; they have very good common sense; they have a natural ability to relate to people; they are empathetic, personable, intuitive, and experienced in helping people work through challenging issues. They have often overcome challenges and adversity themselves, which helps them to guide others with similar issues.

The primary difference between therapists and Life Coaches is that therapists tend to focus more on the past or present (which is very important when working with trauma) while coaches tend to focus more on the present and the future. Therapists analyze their client's past as a tool for understanding present behaviors, whereas Life Coaches identify and describe current problematic behaviors, so the client can work to modify them for lasting positive change. Some find great progress seeing a therapist for past trauma and a coach for accountability.

How do clients typically work with a Life Coach?

When you work with a Life Coach, it typically involves meeting once every one or two weeks for 45–60 minutes over a period of one to six months. Because it can take from thirty to ninety days to change a habit, Life Coaches will want to work with someone for a period of several months for the client to gain maximum results. In addition to the weekly or bi-weekly meetings, most Life Coaches also offer voice, text, or email check-ins in between the meetings. This is helpful because things may come up in our life that we need some guidance to deal with.

Most of my clients have been through my 30 Days to Healthy Living program that changes lives. The benefits are more natural energy, better sleep, weight loss, and healthier lifestyle changes, which all create better eating habits for life.

My approach to coaching

In my experience working with clients, what I have learned is that self-care is probably the most important aspect of self-development. It is especially important for those who are naturally more nurturing to others, who give more energy away than they receive. I believe self-care and self-love is the basis for making any lasting change in your life. And, as a result, I always include that component in my coaching.

Here are some of the self-care tips I like to offer to clients that you can start today as well:

- Create some alone time for yourself even if it's just a few minutes a day
- Do something you love to do, either alone or with friends or family
- Pamper yourself: Get a massage, facial, or acupuncture
- Get some sun and spend time in nature
  o Use Red Light Therapy in the winter
- Ground yourself by placing your feet or body on grass, sand, or in a body of water
  o You can also buy a grounding mat if you prefer to be indoors

- Exercise is also very grounding, and movement is very important to move out stagnant energy
  - Walk, jog, do some jumping jacks, get a rebounder, practice some yoga poses or simple stretching, etc.
- Love Yourself, Nurture Yourself, Accept Yourself, Forgive Yourself
  - There are so many ways to do this, but the best thing is to start. Anything that you do for yourself is a form of self-love
  - Look in the mirror and tell yourself that you love yourself. It can feel a little awkward at first, but it becomes easier
  - Remind yourself of your worth
- Connect to God, the Universe or whatever you believe in
- Pray or write your desires down - It is said a goal or desire not written down is just a dream
- Journal
  - When you look back on your journal entries you will see how much progress you made
  - There are so many different types of journals and some that will even give you writing prompts. Even just writing down what you are grateful for is a great place to start.

- Emotional Freedom Technique
  - o You can either find a coach or therapist to do this with you, or go to YouTube and follow along to some videos

Here are some tips from Ayurveda that I like to recommend for better health:

1. Practice good digestive health – All experiences in life—mental, physical, and emotional—contribute to your digestive health. A healthier diet will lead to improved physical health and also increase happiness and enrich your life in so many ways.
   a. Eat three meals a day
      i. Have a snack between meals if necessary
   b. Avoid snacking and grazing
   c. Chew your food well
   d. Eat your biggest meal at noon
      i. Your Digestive Fire is at its peak at Noon when the sun is the highest in the sky
   e. Eat in a quiet, settled environment and preferably not on the go
      i. When you are relaxed it's much easier for your body to digest and absorb the nutrients

f. Avoid eating when upset, angry or anxious.

    i. You're in a high-stress situation, so your sympathetic nervous system kicks in, making hunger a much smaller priority and suppressing hunger pangs by slowing down your digestion

g. Limit frozen foods

    i. Frozen is better than canned foods, however if you can buy fresh fruits and vegetables that is ideal

h. Limit eat leftovers

    i. Ayurveda believes leftover foods contain ama, which basically means toxicity in Ayurveda. The longer leftovers sit, the more toxic they become due to fermentation by bacteria. Do not heat honey, as it can become toxic. Honey should only be consumed Raw in its natural state

i. Sip warm water throughout the day

    i. Warm water is better absorbed by the body and helps hydrate you

j. Take a short gentle walk after meals

    i. Walking increasing the metabolism

2. Sleeping well – Ayurveda says that being asleep by 10:00 p.m. helps the efficiency of the metabolic processes that occur between 10:00 p.m. and 2:00 a.m. that night. The nutrients you consumed during the day will get assimilated and used for fuel the next day. If you start getting to bed earlier, there will be a noticeable increase in the quality of your life.

    a. Lights out by 9:45 /10 pm
    b. Eat dinner at least three hours before going to bed.
    c. Don't exercise too late at night
    d. Turn your phone off or put on airplane mode across the room when you go to sleep
    e. Put warm oil on your head and feet – lavender is very relaxing
    f. Drink herbal tea

3. Exercise to reduce your risk of pain and injuries – Everyone knows that for optimal health, they need to move their bodies more. Nonetheless, many people are not getting the exercise they need. Try to exercise in the morning so you have sufficient energy. It is also important to exercise based on your dosha.

    a. Vata – Aerobic (20–25 minutes, 4/5 times a week), Strength Training (20 minutes with lighter weights,

3/4 times a week), Daily Yoga (once or twice a day for 10–15 minutes), Pilates

b. Pitta – Aerobic (20–25 minutes, 4/5 times a week), Strength Training (20 minutes with medium weights, 3/4 times a week), Daily Yoga (once or twice a day for 10–15 minutes), Pilates

c. Kapha – Aerobic (30–40 minutes, 4/5 times a week), Strength Training (20 minutes increasing the weights as you become stronger, 3/4 times a week), Daily Yoga (once or twice a day for 10 minutes), Pilates

4. Live within nature's rhythms – When you're in tune with nature's rhythms, you tend to feel better. From the perspective of Ayurveda, the state of health and wholeness comes from living in alignment with the rhythms of nature—that is, following a lifestyle and diet that promote balance throughout the day. Here's an ideal morning routine.

a. Rise early. Ayurveda recommends waking up early before 6:00 a.m.

b. Clear the Channels. Most of us naturally rush to the bathroom to urinate when we first awaken, but it's also helpful to train your body to evacuate the bowels first thing in the morning—or in those first few waking hours.

    c. Clean your mouth. Digestion begins in the mouth. Therefore, it's important to have a clean, fresh mouth so you can taste your food well.

        i. Scraping the tongue in the morning of the Ama, the white residue is a great way to start the day

    d. Stimulate your organs. Drink some warm water with some lemon juice.

    e. Do a soothing self-massage. Anoint your body with warm herbalized oil to balance your doshas, stimulate circulation, enhance muscle tone, calm your mind, enhance well-being, and promote longevity.

    f. Stretch and strengthen. To shake off that early-morning stiffness and tone your muscles, do some gentle yoga asana stretches.

    g. Meditate.

    h. Eat a healthy breakfast.

5. Ayurveda detox – Check out these Ayurveda detoxification methods to reduce ama (toxins) and increase ojas (the essence of pure health). The purpose

of a detox is to give our digestive system rest, so it doesn't need to work so hard breaking down heavy foods.

a. Follow a three-week light diet made up of cooked mung beans, well- cooked vegetables, and a gluten-free grain. You can have cooked fruit as a snack or gluten-free, yeast-free bread. Remember the guideline of 60 percent cooked veggies, 20 percent carbohydrates, and 20 percent protein will also apply during this detox.

b. Do not eat fried food, hot and spicy foods, cold foods or drinks, raw salads, root vegetables, red meat, dairy, alcohol, or sugar during your detox diet. Reduce the amount of coffee you drink. Substitute green tea if you need more energy. You can have a small amount of coconut palm sugar or organic cane sugar if you are used to eating a lot of sugar.

I hope as you read this you can take some time for yourself today, no matter how busy you are. You can only give from what you have, so fill your cup back up daily.

Here are some of the other tools I like to use and recommend in my coaching:

- Meditation
  - o I recommend learning Transcendental Meditation from a certified teacher in your area—Go to www.tm.org or tm-women.org to find a teacher
  - o Otherwise do your own research and see what works for you
- Find your Dharma—Life Purpose through Astrology and Ayurveda
- Customizing the coaching for your Personality Type according to Myers Briggs, Enneagram, Love Languages, etc.
- Customizing the coaching for your lifestyle, short-term and long-term goals

Don't try to change too many things at once. Take one habit and start it daily or weekly and once you have that down, then add another. Especially with our busy lives, we need to start with baby steps and consistency first, otherwise we just get overwhelmed.

I can now see a path forward for me in this exciting field of life coaching, where I can build on the many years of experience

I have as a teacher of meditation and an expert of natural health. I feel I have a great deal to offer to clients and have a diverse set of tools and resources that can help. I have also experienced my own significant adversities in life. Therefore, I can use that experience to help guide you and provide you with the necessary tools to overcome your challenges. My coach would always say: "I'm just a few steps ahead of you!" That always made me feel so relieved.

My offer to you:

I can help you come back home to yourself and help you find your happiness within. It's always been there, even when stress, pain, and trauma have covered it up.

I will help carve out a realistic plan, suitable for your goals, desires, and current lifestyle, which is different for everyone since we are all unique human beings with different needs.

My goal is to help as many people as possible come back home to themselves and feel happy, healthy, and fulfilled. Maharishi Mahesh Yogi said: "The purpose of life is the expansion of happiness". I know that can be hard to believe with all the suffering in the world. His purpose was to help raise the consciousness of the world through TM, which calms the stressed nervous system and expands the mind to its full potential. This state of consciousness is natural to us, but due to all the stress and suffering in the world, it can be overshadowed. You are amazing and deserve the best in life. I hope this book has inspired you to Find Happiness Within. Thank you for reading.

I want to thank my parents, my editor Lisa Thaler, and my boyfriend, and all my family and friends in my life for believing in me. I want to thank my TM students for showing their appreciation towards me over the years. One of my TM students told me recently when I told him I was writing this book that I have an ageless wisdom for one so young. Wow, what a compliment.

About The Author

Olivia Lopez has spent her entire life immersed in the field of natural health and the development of consciousness, both as a student of these fields and as a teacher and coach for others to pursue these areas of knowledge.

Olivia grew up in Albuquerque, New Mexico, until she left at the age of five with her mother to spend ten years of her life in Germany. She returned to the U.S. as a high school student at the Maharishi School in Fairfield, Iowa, where she received a consciousness-based education. After high school, she continued her studies at Maharishi International University, where she received both a B.A. and M.B.A., and deepened her knowledge about natural health and the development of consciousness through Transcendental Meditation.

After her post-graduate studies, Olivia trained over 1,000 students in the Transcendental Meditation program over a period of 10 years, where she taught a wide range of students, from high school students in inner-city schools in San Francisco, to Hollywood celebrities in Beverly Hills, to nurses in Sarasota, Florida, and to the public throughout California and Florida.

Currently, Olivia is a life and business coach who helps her clients live a less stressful, more healthy life by using several tools that are based on her knowledge of natural health.

Printed in the United States
by Baker & Taylor Publisher Services